Volume IV in a series
"Narrow Gauge Railways of Europe"

CLOUDS ON T⌐
BRIENZER R⌐

A BRIEF HISTORY OF ⌐
BRIENZ ROTHORN BAHN

BY
PETER ARNOLD

Plateway Press, PO Box 973, Brighton, BN2 2TG
1 871980 21 6

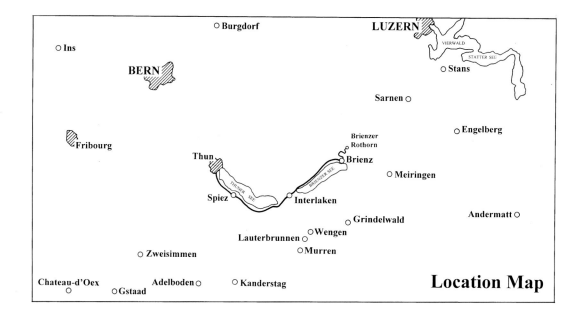

Location Map

Printed in Great Britain by Wayzgoose PLC, Sleaford, Lincs.

ISBN 1 871980 21 6

Cover artwork by John Holroyd

Book design by Keith Taylorson / Martin Snow, Intersoft Multimedia

Front cover illustration:
    BRB 0-4-2T No. 7 climbs away from Planalp with the 14.50 Brienz to Kulm train on 13 August 1964.
                                                                                    (Brian Stephenson)
Frontispiece:
    0-4-2T No. 4 awaits departure at Brienz, 12 August 1961.   *(John K Williams)*

CONTENTS

INTRODUCTION

Without the invention of the steam locomotive, which enabled Switzerland to develop during the nineteenth century, it is certain that tourism would not have increased so rapidly. Without this rapid growth many of the tourist and mountain railways which provide so much pleasure today would not have been built.

One of these railways is the Brienz Rothorn Bahn (BRB) whose survival has depended upon tourists, not always successfully. Indeed it is only because it remained closed during a period when other lines were being converted or built for electric operation that steam still reigns supreme today. After a history of one hundred, sometimes very difficult, years this fascinating line has now entered its second century.

The BRB Company is now more secure financially than ever before but remains determined to preserve its centenarian steam locomotives in daily operation for as long as possible. The Company's success lies in the fact that these old machines which are expensive to operate and maintain now work alongside modern locomotives, both diesel and oil fired steam, which are more economic. A careful balance of both ensures that fares can be maintained at such a level that today's visitors can afford to travel up the Rothorn.

The Brienz Rothorn Bahn relies greatly upon the financial support and patronage of the public and deserves all the help it receives. Throughout the line's history many people have encouraged and assisted the Company in preserving this steam rack railway to enable future generations to witness and experience the culture of a bygone age.

To see steam locomotives working hard in such a beautiful landscape is an increasing rarity in Western Europe and, once experienced, is not easily forgotten. The views both during the journey and from the summit of the Brienzer Rothorn on a clear day are also unforgettable and an experience not to be missed.

My wife and I first visited the Brienzer Rothorn and its railway in 1982. Two years later I purchased a copy of "Dampf am Brienzer Rothorn" ("Steam on the Brienzer Rothorn") by P. Cosandier which was published by BRB in 1983. I eventually managed to translate this booklet which served to whet my appetite to learn more about the railway. Further visits led to 1992 and the BRB's centenary year when we visited the summit at least three times, sometimes by train and sometimes on foot, during our two week holiday. The railway was exceptionally busy and this helped me to make my own video record of trains at work on the Rothorn.

In 1992, to celebrate their centenary year, BRB published "Brienz Rothorn Bahn, Hundert Jahre Kampf um Dampf" (literally, "Brienz Rothorn Bahn's 100 Year Battle for Steam") by Arthur Wüthrich which again I managed to translate. Information from these two publications together with my own observations formed the basis for this book which, to the best of my knowledge, is the first entirely devoted to the railway to be published in this country.

If you are familiar with the Brienz Rothorn Bahn, I hope this book will increase the enjoyment of your next visit. If you have yet to visit the line then I hope I have provided you with enough encouragement to make the trip.

Peter Arnold.
April 1995

Chapter 1
THE FORMATIVE YEARS

Application For The Concession

The Brienzer Rothorn was well known as a beautiful mountain viewpoint long before the coming of its railway. To cater for visitors the first inn was opened on the Eastern ridge in 1838. After being destroyed by fire in 1846, this was replaced by a guest house complete with sleeping and stabling facilities in 1864. About this time a new pony track was built from Brienz via Planalp to the Rothorn summit to encourage further visitors. However this guest house closed in 1874 through lack of custom and also became a victim of fire in 1885.

However by then tourism was beginning to thrive within Switzerland and several people realised that more mountain railways would encourage tourism still further. The Rigi Railway, which opened in 1871, had proved that steam rack locomotives could operate successfully on 1 in 4 gradients. Therefore the people of Brienz decided to form a committee to investigate the possibility of constructing a line to the Rothorn summit.

As a result the application to build a rack railway from Brienz to the Rothorn was submitted by Karl Brück on 15th October 1889, by which time the Pilatus Railway had opened on gradients as steep as 1 in 2. Little is known of Brück except that he was a German involved with the production and marketing of carved woodwork at Brienz, a village famous for this work. Brück was assisted in his application by the German engineer Alexander Lindner who was living in Lucerne. We may never know which of these two originally conceived such a bold plan but it seems that later they may have been involved in a dispute because Brück's name plays little further part in the story.

The Swiss engineer Roman Abt, renowned for his mountain railway rack system who also lived in Lucerne, gave them his support by confirming that the budgeted costs used in their application were sufficient even allowing for the high prices of mechanical equipment then prevailing.

On 20th December, only 65 days after application, the concession was granted by the Swiss National and State authorities. This authorised Karl Brück, industrialist of Brienz, acting on behalf of a committee, to employ someone to form a joint stock company to build and operate a rack railway from Brienz to the Rothorn under certain articles and conditions.

The concession was granted for 80 years provided that plans were approved within 2 years. It defined that the State would decide the railway's speed limit. Fares were not to exceed 10 fr up and 6 fr downhill. Children under 4 years, not occupying a seat, were to travel free. Hand luggage weighing up to 5 kilos was to be free; for a further 10 kilos the charge was to be 50 rappen, and for each kilo above that a further 5 rappen. Goods up to 20 kilos weight were to be charged 60 rappen, increased by 30 rappen for each extra 10 kilos. The Company were permitted to set their own tariff for collection and delivery of goods. It also stipulated that when the Company's profits exceeded 6% within any period of three consecutive years then the fares were to be reduced accordingly. From the outset the Company were ordered to keep sufficient finance in reserve for maintenance and to set up a sickness and welfare fund, or take out insurance, to protect their staff.

Both Brück and Lindner were convinced that the prospect for the line was promising according to their jointly signed document," Presentation for Preparation of a Company for a Rothorn Railway" dated 2nd January 1890. On the same date Lindner wrote his "Memorandum of the Project for a Railway from Brienz to the Rothorn (Berne Canton)" in which he described the advantages that such a line would bring to Brienz and the neighbouring Oberland thus:

> "The mountains around Lake Lucerne have echoed to the sound of the Rigi Railway for 20 years so the construction of another mountain railway will create few problems. However dubious folk may say that there is still some element of risk, but this will be borne by the promoters. The large number of visitors to the mountain who are deceived by its height will find it easier and safer to admire the Alpine scenery by making the difficult ascent by the "steam horse". The Rigi Railway, opened in 1871, has prospered and other mountain viewpoints, whilst retaining their attraction for sportsmen, now have fewer visitors as a result........At an altitude of 2252 metres Rothorn Railway passengers will gain pleasure from obtaining a grand scenic view which is only rarely obscured by mist".

He praised the Pilatus Railway which had carried 37,000 passengers in its opening year in 1889. He also prophesied success for both the Monte Generoso Railway, built by Theodor Bertschinger, and the project for a line up Mount Säntis.

The Rothorn Railway would become not only one of the highest ascents in the world but also that with the greatest difference in altitude from top to bottom. Lindner used the following comparisons:

Mt. Washington	816 - 1909 metres	Pilatus	441 - 2066 metres
Vitznau-Rigi	437 - 1750 metres	Monte Generoso	277 - 1639 metres
Arth-Rigi	421 - 1750 metres	Brienz Rothorn	570 - 2252 metres

Competition

Towards the end of 1890 the fever of mountain railway construction was spreading and various ill conceived schemes were being proposed throughout the Bernese Oberland as some of the following examples demonstrate:

On 14th September the Councillors of Schattenhalb/Meiringen met with the intention of using whatever legal means were necessary to prevent construction of a proposed railway from Grindelwald, over Grosse Scheidegg, to Oberhasli.

On 11th October Mr. Heer-Betrix of Biel, who from 1888-91 was a co-promoter of the Mürren and Wengernalp Railways, applied for a line to the Wetterhorn and another from Lauterbrunnen to Visp through a tunnel in the Lötschental.

In December an application for the Lötschberg Railway was made by Wilhelm Teuscher, a State and National Councillor for Därstetten, under the leadership of Bühler, the National Councillor for Frutigen.

The Schynige-Platte Company submitted plans for a "super railway" to the 4158 metre Jungfrau which was believed to be no problem because previously there had been a proposal to link the peaks of Finsteraarhorn and Oldenhorn with a balloon cableway!

The members of the Rothorn Railway committee, under Brück as President and Lindner as Engineer, were wary of any neighbouring schemes and were determined to face up to any competition. On 30th November they learnt of an application for a line with a route from the Brünig Railway at Brünig via the Rothorn, down to Brienz and on to Interlaken. The proposal included a similar route as their own and was estimated to cost 3.9m.fr. The application included the following words:

"The Rothorn Railway will be a "dead end" railway and will have to rely purely upon tourist traffic whereas this railway will have other advantages. Passengers from Lucerne to Interlaken will have the benefit, with little extra travelling time, of going via the highest mountain yet conquered by a railway which will provide them with views of both the lowlands and the giant mountains of the Bernese Oberland".

Brienz (Berner Oberland)

HOTEL KREUZ & POST (Dampfschiff-Restauration)
Gegenüber dem Brünig- und Rothornbahnhof, sowie am Landungsplatz der Dampfboote. Grosser schattiger Garten.
Familie E. Hanauer, Propr.

Eiger Mönch Jungfrau

Brienz-Rothorn-Bahn
Berner-Oberland.

Chapter 2
THE BUILDERS

Theodor Bertschinger

Theodor Bertschinger, contractor for the Brienz Rothorn Railway, was born in Lenzburg on 30th March 1845. He was educated at the Canton School in Aarau before going on to Karlsruhe Technical College in 1863. He later studied building at Zurich College before commencing apprenticeship as a carpenter. However he did not enjoy this work and turned to construction after only eight weeks.

In Spring 1866, he decided to try and earn his own living. Together with his brother Otto, he went to Lausanne but found little work there, as was also the case later in Neuchatel. After only a few weeks lodging in a guest house in the village of Travers, where the other guests proved too fond of insobriety, he moved to Vevey where he found work in an architect's office at a monthly salary of 80 fr. But the 22 year old was eager to learn more so he travelled to Paris.

There he soon found work with an architect at a monthly salary of 125 fr and did a lot of work for the Paris Exhibition. He had an enjoyable nine months in the French capital even though he was restricted financially. At the beginning of December 1867 he retraced his steps to Lenzburg where he started his own construction business with 500 fr of his own money and a loan of 1,000 fr.

At last Bertschinger found delight in being able to create his own designs. Thanks to his aptitude and perseverance he was able to take on 30 employees in his first year of business. Business flourished, perhaps helped by his firm belief that God was always on hand to help

1.   Contractor, Theodor Bertschinger
(courtesy BRB)

him overcome any problem. He then turned to railway construction but his first work, the Seetal Railway, brought many problems. The Company went bankrupt and he was only able to collect his debt of 200,000 fr after many years of struggle. This job was followed by several other large railway projects.

During 1890/91 Theodor Bertschinger lived in Brienz whilst he and Alexander Lindner constructed the Rothorn Railway. Despite making excellent progress the Company was faced with a shortfall of 350,000 fr due to a banking crisis in 1891. Having received no payment the two men acquired the Company, together with its debts, in 1892. The Company continued to operate at a loss and they were unable to form the new Joint Stock Company, in which each of them held shares of 200,000 fr, until 1900.

In 1908, despite suffering from gout, Theodor Bertschinger won a contract worth 600,000 fr for building the new Lauterbrunnen - Wengen line. After good progress the contract was completed by November 1909, although unfortunately five men were killed in several accidents. However a landslide occurred a few months later which entailed his return to Wengen to make repairs before the line could reopen on 5th July 1910.

Bertschinger was a District Councillor in Lenzburg and a Member of the Cantonal Parliament until 1910. He died in 1911.

Alexander Lindner

Alexander Lindner was born in 1839 in Coburg, Saxony, now Bavaria. He received a good training in Germany whilst employed with engineering companies working on various railway projects. He acted as engineer for the Gotthard Railway and also, from 1894, during construction of Lucerne station. Before his move to Brienz he was chief engineer to the International Society of Mountain Railways based in Aarau. He became particularly fascinated by the technical problems involved in building mountain lines.

Lindner was a most conscientious planner with a good understanding of practical problems. When he needed a contractor for one of his projects he always ensured that he employed one of first class calibre. During their time together at Brienz, Lindner and Bertschinger ensured that they issued all instructions themselves to ensure that their wishes were met. It was said that all the staff at Brienz were made well aware that unsatisfactory performance would not be tolerated.

Lindner was in demand as an expert adviser and became known for his various technical papers concerning rack railway points and systems and in 1879 wrote a book about the system to calculate the effective length of mountain railways. This he calculated by comparing the horizontal length of a railway with its gradient. By taking into account frictional losses from gradients and curves, the required locomotive power can be found. Thus he was able to calculate not only the effective length but also coal consumption and maintenance costs to determine the scale of fares for passengers and goods. For the 7.6 km Rothorn Railway he calculated the effective length to be 46.7 km.

Lindner left nothing to chance when planning his route up the Rothorn. Terrain, subsoil and avalanche protection were all carefully investigated so as to decide the optimum siting of the line. A deviation towards the south through a tunnel at Oberstafel would have given passengers a majestic Alpine panoramic view over Lake Brienz at the tunnel exit. He rejected this both because of the unstable geological formation and on financial grounds.

2. Engineer, Alexander Lindner
(courtesy BRB)

Most of Lindner's plans, together with his cost calculations for the bridges, have survived and confirm his knowledge and accuracy. The Lindner and Bertschinger partnership built the line exactly as planned resulting in an interesting and successful asset for the company to operate. Even if not agreeing with their commercial forecasts, one has to respect the quality of their work. The sheer boundless enthusiasm with which the pair went to work was matched by many other railway builders throughout Switzerland around the turn of the century.

During his stay of about ten years in Brienz, Lindner became involved with other projects in the area. He devised a way of providing a Winter service between Giswil and Meiringen on the Brünig Railway. He also designed the Harder Funicular at Interlaken which opened in 1908 despite opposition from environmentalists who feared that such view points would become despoiled by new hotels catering for the growth in tourism.

From 1892 Alexander Lindner managed the operation of the Rothorn Railway and helped in forming the new Joint Stock Company whereupon he handed over daily responsibility in 1900.

3.   This early commercial postcard shows the topography of the Rothorn and surrounding peaks to good advantage. *(collection Keith Taylorson)*

Chapter 3
CONSTRUCTION AND OPENING

Choice Of Route

Alexander Lindner made allowance in his profit forecast that the Brünig Railway would not open from Brienz to Interlaken for some time and in fact this did not occur until 1916. However in 1890 an engineer named Pümpin did seek permission to build a line along the south bank of Lake Brienz to connect Interlaken with Kienholz. This plan failed when it met with fierce opposition from environmentalists. At Whitsun 1988 this route was opened not for a railway but for a motorway much of which is in tunnel!

The footpath from Brienz via Planalp to the Rothorn probably dated from around 1860 and was used for the route of the railway. Alexander Lindner found this an ideal choice for his route even though he judged the terrain to be far less favourable than that on the Rigi. However this disadvantage was outweighed by the technical advances which had been made during the intervening decade.

Lindner discarded the idea of a horizontally mounted rack although one was successfully in use on the Pilatus Railway. He did consider operation by cable but decided that it would be too expensive to operate and would cause anxiety to passengers. He chose the Abt rack system for the line and, as the gradient was to start immediately from Brienz station, there was no need for a mixed rack and adhesion system. A gauge of 80 cm was adopted which allowed the use of 60 metre radius curves. This also meant that the route could be constructed more easily and more cheaply through the landscape.

4. **Construction train in Wang Forest below Geldried.** *(courtesy BRB)*

9

Land Acquisition

The Company had received permission to purchase all the necessary land but their negotiations with the Planalp Alpine Farming Co-operative took some time. However in July 1890 the Co-operative did agree to sell land to the Company for 5,500 fr. This land was needed for building the railway, station layout and station building. For a further 1,500 fr, the Company also purchased just under 2 acres of land on the ridge near Rothorn Kulm for the site of an inn. The Railway also paid 2,000 fr to the Co-operative for the "inconvenience".

The sale agreement stipulated that the Co-operative was forbidden to sell wood carvings, flowers and suchlike nor run an inn in competition. However the Company did agree to carry the Co-operative's milk and milk products

5. Schwarzfluh Tunnel soon after completion   *(courtesy BRB)*

10

6. Loco No.2 taking water on a construction train at Geldried, obviously then the "head of steel", prior to the loop being laid. This scene must be during Spring 1891 because trains were able to reach Planalp by the late Summer. Little has changed here during the last hundred years. *(courtesy BRB)*

at a third of their normal rates. The Railway Company were required to keep open the pony track leading to Entlebuch, which crossed the route at Planalp, and to erect proper lineside fencing on the Co-operative's land together with a suitable number of crossings over the line. They were also contracted to install drainage for control of excess water from the surrounding mountainsides.

Construction work started in Summer 1890 and soon a brisk and colourful way of life was in full swing on the mountain with a labour force of 640 Italians housed in temporary barracks and old mountain huts. Some of their materials and food supplies were carried up by mules but much had to brought up on their own shoulders until work was advanced enough for the use of locomotives and wagons. Work was carried out surprisingly quickly and without any serious accident occurring. A train load of materials was able to climb to the midway station of Hausstadt at Planalp before the end of Summer 1891 and a train reached the summit by 31st October.

Construction Costs

Six tunnels were planned with a total length of 860 metres (actually 690 m when built) at a cost of 273,420 fr. Other estimated costs included six large bridges @ 84,000 fr; 6,740 metres of brickwork @ 121,320 fr and foundations @ 223,240 fr. Further costs were 8.9 km of ballast @ 48,000 fr; 9 km of track @ 567,000 fr; 18 sets of points @ 18,000 fr; turntable at Brienz @ 12,000 fr; 4 water stations with reservoirs @ 10,000 fr; buildings @ 88,000 fr and land purchase @ 55,000 fr. Project management costs were estimated at 66,000 fr whilst 120,000 fr were allowed for interest charges. The cost of the four locomotives was 42,000 fr each, two open carriages @ 7,500 fr each, two closed carriages @ 8,500 fr each, and two open goods wagons @ 3,500 fr each. The estimate for provision of a telegraph system to connect the five stations was 7,000 fr.

7.   A construction train at the lower end of Geldried quite possibly taken on the same day as the previous
     scene. Again little has changed - even the farm building behind the loco is there.   *(courtesy BRB)*

8.   Planalp Station under construction probably about September 1891 as the track has been laid. The
     two storey building has long since disappeared.   *(courtesy BRB)*

9. A down train crossing the original Chüemad Bridge. The carriage next to the loco is almost certainly today's B21. The bridge collapsed in Spring 1942 after being damaged by an avalanche during the preceding Winter. *(courtesy BRB)*

The entire cost of the railway was estimated as 2m.fr and this was later raised to 2.2m.fr although the final sum which Lindner and Bertschinger received for the construction was 1.8m.fr.

	francs			francs
		/	Buildings & Facilities	
		/	Buildings	88,000
Project & Planning		/	Points, Turntable	
Project Management	66,000	/	& Water Facilities	40,000
Interest	120,000	/	Rolling Stock	
Land Purchase	55,000	/	4 Steam Locos	168,000
Track		/	2 Open Carriages	15,000
Foundations	344,560	/	2 Closed Carriages	17,000
Tunnels	273,420	/	2 Goods Wagons	7,000
Bridges	84,000	/	Spare Parts	13,000
Ballast	48,000	/	Various	
Rails & Rack	567,000	/	Stations & Depot	12,000
		/	Reserves	82,020
		/	Total Cost	2,000,000

10. **A gang of construction workmen posing at the lower entrance of Chüemad Tunnel. Note temporary track.** *(courtesy BRB)*

Opening Ceremony 1892

The railway opened on Thursday 17th June 1892 despite official invitations being printed showing Thursday 16th! A steamer was arranged to leave Interlaken at 5.20am to convey the guests to Brienz but there were few early risers. It seemed that the BRB was to be left wanting for passengers from the very start! However Brienz village was bedecked with festive flags and, despite rain, crowds came from throughout the area to watch invited guests arriving at the station. At 9.30am the 70 or 80 escorted guests travelled up the mountain in two trains.

Upon reaching the summit the cold drizzle ensured that views in every direction were completely hidden by mist and clouds which made the guests hurry into the temporary restaurant. A speech was made by the Bernese Supreme Officer who greeted the festive crowd on behalf of the management. Alexander Lindner and Theodor Bertschinger were presented with laurel wreaths in appreciation of the thanks for their excellent work.

After travelling back down to Brienz, a formal banquet was held later at the Giessbach Hotel on the south side of Lake Brienz.

Chapter 4
EARLY YEARS OF OPERATION

Debts

Presentation of the railway's financial affairs was as bad as the construction had been good. The report to shareholders of the first year's operation showed a large shortfall in payments for share purchases. 352,100 fr of the original 1.2m.fr share capital remained unpaid at the end of 1891 and a year later 185,000 fr were still outstanding! Several people who had promised to purchase shares could not be traced or had simply gone bankrupt whilst others had retracted and were disputing payment for various reasons. Rather than following up all these debtors through the respective district courts, the Company instituted legal proceedings for the larger debts in the Federal Court.

The Company owed Lindner and Bertschinger 274,559.10 fr at the end of 1892 in addition to which the council and inhabitants of Brienz were suing the railway in respect of damage to the forests. It was intended that the amount of the summons should be decided by the local magistrates because agreement of the amount with the Company could not be reached. The railway held the construction enterprise responsible and vice versa. Because of the shortage of funds, building work ceased on the summit hotel. In order to satisfy travellers a simple inn was established until the hotel could be completed.

Lindner and Bertschinger were obliged, under their contract, to manage the railway's operation for the first two months. In the railway's interest, this was extended into 1893. Indeed because of the depth of the insolvency Alexander Lindner managed the daily operations himself. Despite this the railway went bankrupt.

Miscalculations

In his financial projection for the Rothorn Railway Lindner had assumed 25,000 passengers per year at a fare of 16 fr with operating costs of 103,000 fr. Allowing for interest payments @ 4.5% on the 800,000 fr investment capital already received, he calculated that the gross income should reach not less than 21.7% (= 261,000 fr) of the 1.2m.fr share capital! He did in fact also make calculations based on 18,000 passengers, and only 12,000 as the worst possibility, which would have provided income of 13.6% (= 163,200 fr) and 6.7% (= 80,400 fr) respectively. Later he revised these figures still lower!

Lindner's passenger calculations of 1890 also proved to be over optimistic. The Vitznau-Rigi Railway had carried an average of 86,155 passengers per year between 1871 and 1888, the Arth-Rigi Railway 37,431 between 1875 and 1888, and the Uetliberg Railway 68,189 in the same period. With these figures in mind he believed that mountain railways in the heart of Switzerland would develop even more rapidly. He compared Brienz with Vitznau on Lake Lucerne where one in six people who arrived by lake steamer transferred to the Rigi Railway. The comparative figure for Brienz was 97,000 passengers per year and so Lindner expected 16,000 passengers to transfer to his Rothorn trains.

At first he hoped that further passengers would arrive via the Brünig Railway, originally opened from Alpnachstad to Brienz on 14th June 1888, which was extended into Lucerne on 1st June 1889, the same day that the Pilatus Railway commenced operation. But all too soon Lindner's incorrect assumptions became apparent!

The Company's financial report of 3rd April 1893 stated that, in accordance with the issue conditions, payments for 450,000 fr in shares and 150,000 fr in bonds had already been promised and thus had been excluded from the offer for subscription - in fact only 170,000 fr cash was received. The remaining 750,000 fr in shares and 850,000 fr in 4.5% bonds were subscribed for at par. It was originally reported that the issued bond capital had been oversubscribed by 3 times and that of the shares by 87 times and it was now apparent that the Rothorn Railway's initial subscription had not been as successful as stated!

Under New Ownership

Lindner and Bertschinger finally gained ownership of the railway in 1893 and completed the summit hotel with 32 beds the following year.

Lindner's most pessimistic forecast of 12,000 passengers per year was never attained. In the opening year of 1892 there had been 5,568 passengers which resulted in a loss of 4,638.80 fr. The new owners' losses continued year after year from at worst 23,388 fr in 1894 to at best 3,657 fr in 1898, when over 7,000 passengers were carried for the first time.

Brienz Parish Council minutes for 20th January 1894 reported that, due to the circumstances, the manager of the BRB had been unable to pay the rates for 1893 and that a complaint was to be made to the Federal Court.

After obtaining a lease for a yearly rent of 500 fr in 1899, Lindner lived in the four roomed house owned by Jean Zehndr until after the turn of the century. Zehndr was the senior loco driver and, from 17th October 1913, became depot manager of the railway.

PASSENGER FIGURES 1892 - 1899

1892......5,568	/	1896......3,983
1893......4,281	/	1897......5,516
1894......4,652	/	1898......7,548
1895......6,470	/	1899......5,293

Station Brienz (1892)

11. **Brienz Station soon after opening in 1892 with No.4 waiting for passengers. By comparing this view with that in illust. 39, the building alterations of 1935 are plain to see.**   *(courtesy BRB)*

Chapter 5
DIFFICULT YEARS

A New Company

Under the leadership of Brigadier Matthaus Zurbuchen (1845-1902), who was the Ringgenberg Public Prosecutor and a National Councillor, a new joint stock company with a fully paid share capital of 700,000 fr was formed in 1900 to promote the railway and hotel company under the daily management of Messrs. Hirt and Briner. The new Brienz Rothorn Bahn Company acquired the assets from Lindner and Bertschinger for the sum of 625,000fr although both men remained as shareholders. The new company's first year of operation resulted in a loss of 24,801.26 fr. In the 1900 business report the wars in South Africa and China together with the high cost of coal were blamed for this loss. The lack of a rail connection from Brienz to Interlaken was blamed as another contributory factor.

Operations Until World War I

The heavy snowfalls of Winter 1901/02 caused large clearance costs involving wages for 60 men. However the blame for another poor year in 1902 was attributed to the lack of English visitors, due to repeated postponement of King Edward VII's Coronation, together with the bad state of the German economy. On 30th April 1903 a special train conveyed a party of thirty English VIP's up as far as Planalpfluh Tunnel. For the first time the annual accounts showed a profit, of 1,906.53 fr. The directors reported that the fourth year of operation (since formation of the new company) had at last brought a halt to the chronic losses and provided more hope for the future.

However a further loss of 8,351.03 fr was recorded in 1904. In an attempt to attract more passengers a sixteen metre length of the Planalpfluh Tunnel wall was opened out to provide a scenic attraction. Also during 1904 the Company managed to cancel a forestry agreement which had been made with the Canton in 1891. The idea of this scheme had been to promote tree growth, higher up the mountain in the Schöngütsch area, in an effort to reduce the amount of storm debris carried down by the streams which caused flooding in the valley.

Following further large snowfalls during the Winter, operation in 1906 commenced after a tunnel had been cut through a 12 metre deep drift in the cutting at the entrance to Chüemad Tunnel. This ice cavern, which did not start melting until the middle of July, was a source of delight to the passengers. Thanks to a magnificent Summer the Bernese Oberland saw a tremendous increase in foreign visitors and the growth in the railway's traffic was believed to have been caused by passengers recommending their friends to make the journey.

1907 proved to be even better with 15,589 passengers carried; indeed on Sunday 4th August 1,101 people were transported up the mountain! Despite operating income of 56,500 fr for the year, the result was an overall loss of 1,500 fr.

The line received a setback in 1908 after an avalanche badly damaged the bridge over the Mühle Stream at Chüemad which cost the Company 6,622.40 fr in unforeseen repairs. Poor weather, the strained political position, market and economy crises, high prices and increased competition led to a large decline in traffic resulting in a loss of over 15,000 fr. In order to recoup a little of this loss a locomotive and two goods wagons were hired out in December 1908 and January 1909 to contractors building the Montreux - Glion Railway. Theodor Bertschinger became President of the BRB in November 1908.

In 1909 the Company managed to secure a loan of 20,000 fr by pledging the summit hotel as security. After a break of one year, an evening train was reintroduced in 1910 on which one could travel up and stay overnight in the hotel for 15 fr, later reduced to 10 fr. Traffic for 1910 was the new Company's second worst, due once again to poor Summer weather, and the railway slipped closer towards insolvency. Shareholders voted to accept a further loan of 70,000 fr from which Berne Canton withheld 20,000 fr as security against their earlier loan. The BRB was still not considered to be credit worthy!

The unexpected death of the Company President, Theodor Bertschinger, on 27th May 1911 dealt another blow. In the same year the BRB purchased a loco on very favourable terms from the recently electrified Wengernalp Railway. The cost for this loco, which became No.5 in the BRB fleet, was 2,200 fr including delivery plus another 5,500 fr for necessary modifications. The weather favoured the railway during 1911 and the directors proudly noted that revenue from the railway and hotel operations had produced a surplus of 1,773.04 fr.

During 1912 Eduard Seiler, hotelier of Interlaken, became a director and negotiated unsuccessfully for a sale of the Company to the consortium which owned the Giessbach Hotel. Although no banks were prepared to lend more money to the BRB, the Lakes Thun and Brienz Steamship Company were. They were ready to grant a loan of 30,000 fr in return for pledges of the railway and hotel. However the hotel was already pledged against the earlier loans.

The Lake Thun Railway Company succeeded the Steamship Company as from 1st July 1912. After yet another merger on 1st January 1913, the Bernese Alpine company, Bern-Lötschberg-Simplon (BLS), took over the lake steamer operations. In the same year the name of the station at Hausstadt was changed to Planalp after being agreed under oath with the Swiss Railway Department. Brienz Parish Council granted a contribution of 915.15 fr to clear the debts of 1912/13 which reduced the operating loss to 700 fr.

The Company report for 1914 was dramatic:

"As a result of the outbreak of war it was agreed with the Transport Union Institution on 5th August that the late season timetable could be introduced. However traffic dropped almost to nothing and so on the evening of 9th August, the day of introduction of war timetables on other lines, our operations were suspended".

The railway employed 23 people, not including the six paid on a daily basis during Winter, all of whom were given notice. This action, which did not include the head of operations who remained in employment, led to problems in 1923.

PASSENGER FIGURES 1900 - 1914

1900.......7,467 / 1905......11,707 / 1910.......9,140

1901.......9,825 / 1906......13,862 / 1911......15,670

1902......11,025 / 1907......15,589 / 1912......10,430

1903......11,275 / 1908......12,673 / 1913......11,652

1904......13,191 / 1909......11,912 / 1914.......4,824

Brienz-Rothorn-Bahn.   **FAHRPLAN PRO SOMMER 1909**   **Brienz-Rothorn-Bahn.**

Gültig vom Tage der Betriebs-Eröffnung an bis 30. September 1909.

STATIONEN	°101	1	•3	5	7	9	11	
Luzern......ab	—	—	—	5.55	7.43	9.52	12.52	•2.20
Meiringen .. »	5.20	5.20	•8.00	9.10	10.53	1.35	4.03	•5.15
Brienz......an	5.43	5.43	•8.23	9.33	11.17	1.58	4.25	•5.35
Bern ....ab	—	—	5.21	†6.45	8.40	11.00	11.00	1.50
Interl.-Brienzers. »	—	5.45	•8.05	8.47	10.42	12.55	2.35	•4.00
Giessbach... »	—	7.04	•8.47	10.01	11.32	2.00	3.51	•5.15
Brienz ..... an	—	7.17	•9.05	10.18	11.47	2.15	4.10	•5.27
Brienz ......ab	°5.45	7.22	•9.07	10.20	11.56	2.17	5.50	
Hausstatt .... »	°6.18	7.55	•9.40	10.53	12.29	2.50	6.23	
Rothorn-Kulm an	°6.55	8.32	•10.17	11.30	1.06	3.27	7.00	

STATIONEN	2	°102	4	•6	8	10	•12	12a
Rothorn-Kulm ab	7.20	°8.37	10.18	•11.30	2.15	3.27	•4.37	▯5.24
Hausstatt... »	7.53	°9.10	10.51	•12.03	2.48	4.00	•5.10	°5.57
Brienz.......an	8.25	°9.42	11.23	•12.35	3.20	4.32	•5.42	▯6.29
Brienz......ab	•8.30	9.44	11.27	•12.50	3.23	•4.35 ▯4.35	•5.45	7.45
Giessbach... »	•8.40	9.51	11.37	•1.00	3.33	•4.47 ▯4.45	•5.57	8.00
Interl.-Brienzers. an	•9.55	11.07	12.35	•1.55	4.40	•5.48 ▯5.55	6.57	9.14
Bern .... »	12.42	1.08	4.07	5.27	7.16	7.50	9.20	†11.00
Brienz......ab	•9.15	10.30	11.58	•1.15	4.25	•5.35	6.45	6.45
Meiringen...an	•9.35	10.53	12.20	•1.35	4.48	•5.57	7.07	7.07
Luzern...... »	•12.22	1.50	3.20	•4.17	7.50	—	9.55	9.55

Zeichenerklärung: * Vom 1. Juli bis und mit 15. September.
† Nur an Sonntagen vom 1. Juli bis 15. Sept.

o Nur Sonntags Juli und August.   ▯ Bis 30. Juni und vom 16. September an.

Brienz 571 m ü. M. — Rothorn-Kulm 2351 m ü. M. — Zahnradbahn, 25%/o Maximalsteigung. Unvergleichlich schöne Bahnfahrt. Grandioses Hochgebirgspanorama. Bezauberndes Schauspiel des Sonnen-Auf- und Niederganges. **Hotel Rothorn-Kulm** mit vorzüglicher Restauration. Sehr mässige Preise.

TARIF: Brienz-Rothorn und zurück Fr. 10.—, General-Abonnemente und Rundreisebillete 20%/o Ermässigung, Sonntagsbillete Fr. 5.— *Gesellschaften und Schulen zu bedeutend reduzierten Taxen. Kombiniertes Billet für Bahn und Hotel à Fr. 15.—, berechtigend zur Bergfahrt mit dem letzten Zuge, Talfahrt beliebig, samt Souper, Logement und Déjeuner im Hotel Rothorn-Kulm.*

Chapter 6
THE PERIOD OF CLOSURE

The First World War

During 1915 the summit hotel remained in operation if only to serve the greatly reduced numbers of climbers whilst the BRB directors took steps towards trying to reopen the railway. With the 1st World War raging they applied to Brienz Council for a loan of 15,000 fr but were offered only 5,000 fr, which was insufficient. To add to their misfortune another avalanche had badly damaged the bridge at Chüemad during the Winter of 1914/15. The management, whilst appreciating the difficulties of the depression, stated that without support the line's future was becoming more uncertain.

At an extraordinary meeting held on 29th January 1916 the BRB directors made a further call for help to Brienz Council for a loan of 20,000 fr, or an advance of 10,000 fr, to ensure survival but they found little sympathy. As a result the Swiss Department of Transport granted a lapse of the operating concession until the end of 1923. Despite this a majority of Brienzers still thought that the line should be saved. However it was unanimously agreed at a meeting on 27th May that the Council should grant a loan to the BRB provided that the BLS joined in with an equal amount. As a result the directors informed their shareholders on 3rd July that the question of demolition could not be decided until the outcome of this offer was known.

On 23rd August the new railway between Brienz and Interlaken was opened but the BRB was not going to be able to take advantage of this until 1931. War still raged and the tourist trade was almost negligible. During 1916 Interlaken Tourist Office recorded a figure for overnight accommodation bookings only 12.8% of those made during the last pre-war year. Demolition of the Rothorn Railway, to provide scrap metal for the ever increasingly expensive demands of war, seemed only a question of time. Although the line was not directly threatened by warfare, the War was still a threat to the railway's future!

The threat of demolition had barely passed in 1917 when Walo Bertschinger, son of the line's builder, acting on behalf of his brothers and sisters proposed that the Company be liquidated and the railway demolished. He believed that whatever could be saved, should be accomplished by the sale of scrap metal. His idea loosed a storm of indignation throughout the Bernese Oberland and in the press. The Council demanded legal custody of the line because they feared that demolition would endanger the village and its church should the route and its walls fall into disrepair. Whilst this fear may have been overstated, it was generally believed that some danger would result. Bertschinger's hopes were dashed when his proposal was defeated by eight votes.

The BLS representative requested that financial provision should be made towards reopening after the end of the War and in fact many people had invested over 8,000 fr per year towards the costs of reopening. As a result, essential maintenance was carried out during the remainder of the closure period.

Successful timber transport was made possible in 1918 as far as Planalp. Other railways had suffered large losses during these poor years, as for example 25,000 fr by the Pilatus Railway in 1917. At least the BRB had been aware of the need for economy and paradoxically had saved money by complete closure.

The Struggle To Reopen

Reopening could still not be considered because coal prices and wages had risen steeply during the War and foreign tourists had not yet returned to the area. In 1900 the average wage had been 45 rappen per hour with bread costing 38 rappen per kilogram. By 1920 a labourer in the Bernese Oberland was earning about 1.46 fr per hour and paying 75 rappen per kilogram for bread. Twice a request for a grant of 50,000 fr towards further repair costs had been declined by the Bernese Government who thought that there was no urgency for recommencing operations.

Brienz Council pointed out that they did not have enough faith in the BRB to meet their request of a mortgage merely by repayment of the 20,000 fr loan with rent and compound interest unless the Company agreed to cede the Summit Hotel property together with the right of repurchase at cost price within five years. In fact this was arranged.

The BRB Company had agreed to pay their redundant employees from the 1914 closure date to the end of that season but had pointed out that they would not be able to afford this until the end of their next season of operations. These men were still awaiting their wages and so Heinrich Nageli, former chief loco driver, wrote to the Swiss Department of Transport on 29th May 1923 to seek help.

After contacting the Company to ascertain the situation, the Department replied on 29th September that the Company did agree the men's claim, which so far they had been unable to pay, and that their original promise would be honoured in due course. The Department also informed Nageli that the Company had been attempting to arrange a sale of the railway and hotel to a large foreign travel consortium but that these negotiations had recently reached an unsuccessful conclusion. That was the end of the matter so far as the Department of Transport were concerned as the matter was beyond their authority. Whether the staff ever reached satisfaction remains unrecorded.

In order to gain income, no matter how small, the BRB hired first one then two carriages to the Schynige-Platte Railway in 1924 and 1925. Because the BRB had not managed to get out of debt and had been unable to make large investments, their line remained the only one still steam operated in the Bernese Oberland. The directors noted this fact with some pride in 1925.

Brienz did not intend to give up its little railway to foreign control. 285 citizens attended a parish meeting on 10th August 1928 and donated a total of 55,000 fr to assist in reopening the railway! From this the Council deducted 5,000 fr which they had advanced earlier that year to pay for urgent repair works. Viktor Rösti, the railway foreman, together with 16 men had worked for a total of 1800 hours to clear part of the route which had become buried.

Far more than the 50,000 fr donated by the Brienzers was required. With wholehearted enthusiasm and sheer determination, the main shareholders, Walo Bertschinger, Adolf Briner-Fischer and Robert Hirt who were men of great influence, negotiated with the BLS to try to arrange further credit against the 50,000 fr already obtained. The negotiations culminated in the BLS director flatly refusing to meet the Brienzers in his office!

Meanwhile the Council had set up a committee to investigate ways and means of refloating the Company. Active participants were the Brienzers Albert Eggler, notary, and Gerhard Hirsch, businessman who both became known as the "new builders" of the BRB Company. After many setbacks they finally received a letter of authorisation from the State.

12. **During the BRB's period of closure Brienz continued to be served by the SBB and by lake steamers. Supplied in 1914 the "Lötschberg", was the last steam ship to be built by Escher Wyss of Zurich. Her inclined 450 hp 2 cylinder superheated compound engine is powered from her two original boilers which were later converted from coal to oil firing.** *(John K Williams)*

New Financial Arrangements

In a document dated 1st August 1930 Albert Eggler certified that: "following their application Peter Grossmann, construction engineer of Brienz, Vice President and Fritz Rösti, of St. Stephen in Brienz, Secretary of Brienz Parish Council have been appointed as the committee for reopening the BRB, and following accurate personal examination of the relative original stock, 222,100 fr has been subscribed for new preference shares".

In addition to the 50,000 fr already described, local citizens, businesses and various other bodies subscribed a further 52,400 fr. Twelve other parishes within the Oberland subscribed 23,300 fr and another 96,400 fr came from elsewhere.

The railway was one step nearer rescue! After achieving this target, the committee sent out around 20,000 copies of the prospectus. Further costs of reopening were 116,098 fr for repairs to rolling stock and buildings plus other general restoration costs of around 9,000 fr.

That success was finally obtained is thanks to the BLS, Brienz Council and not least the functionaries, who during these times of greatest need, had performed work at their own expense!

On 30th August a shareholders' meeting in the Kreuz Hotel at Brienz agreed that the former 1900 share capital of 700,000 fr should be replaced by a new reduced share capital of 140,000 fr. An issue of further shares was to raise another 348,000 fr but problems were to continue until this could be accomplished.

Firstly a consortium from Zurich offered to purchase the hotel from Brienz Council for 11,600 fr in order to provide increased reserves for the railway's operation. This offer was not taken up because the consortium wanted the Council to install avalanche protection above Planalp station. An avalanche had caused destruction there on the night of 7/8th December 1919 but the replacement defences were not built until 1939.

"Schweizerisches Handelsamtsblatt", the official Swiss trade newspaper, reported details in its issue of 11th June 1931:

"On 9th June the joint stock company of the Brienz Rothorn Company announced that, as a result of a decision made at a General Meeting on 30th August 1930, its Articles of Association have been revised.

The share capital of 700,000 fr has been amended to 140,000 fr by reducing the nominal value of 600 preference and 800 ordinary shares from 500 fr to 100 fr. These shares together with newly issued shares form the new 488,000 fr share capital.

The following new shares have been issued:

     500 preference A shares @ 100 fr = 50,000 fr

     2350 preference B shares @ 100 fr = 235,000 fr

     630 ordinary shares @ 100 fr = 63,000 fr

The Company has purchased the summit hotel together with fixtures and fittings from Brienz Council for 35,000 fr. The Board of Directors will consist of from 9 to 11 members. This committee is composed of:

Albert Eggler, notary of Brienz. President.

Walo Bertschinger of Lenzburg, engineer in Zurich.

Adolf Briner-Fischer of Zurich, businessman in Zurich.

Robert Hirt-Bachofen of Schaffhausen, businessman in Regensberg.

Adolf Muhlemann of Bönigen, architect in Interlaken.

Johann Werder of Birrenlauf, hotelier in Interlaken.

Eugen Labhardt of Steckborn, district director for SBB in Lucerne.

Gerhard Hirsch of Brienz, businessman.

Viktor Schneiter of Brienz, manufacturer.

Otto Rohner of Walzenhausen, businessman in Brienz.

The Operations Managers are Gerhard Hirsch, Robert Hirt & Albert Eggler.

The joint signatories for the Company are Gerhard Hirsch & Robert Hirt.

The former signatories of Jakob Ammann & Eduard Seiler are no longer valid".

Chapter 7
BACK IN BUSINESS

Reopening In 1931

Theodor Bertschinger's skill as a master builder and his foresight were such that, despite the railway's seventeen years of closure between 1914 and 1931, he probably saved the railway. The line had been so well built that, despite the passage of time, only minor damage had occurred.

On 9th June 1931 a steam locomotive once again reached the summit but only after tremendous snowdrifts had been cleared from the route. A snow tunnel some 72 metres long was an added attraction for the numerous visitors who would soon appear.

Saturday 13th June was the day of reopening. A local reporter suggested that the day should have been officially declared a holiday but the schools were not given one! The local population had decorated their houses with flags. Another reporter described how the whole of the Swiss press was represented with both sides of the track lined with tripods, cameras and cine cameras. Ceremonial canon fire resounded from up in Haslital and from down in Bödeli (Interlaken) as the first train pounded away towards the Rothorn at 10am. There were more shots at Planalp whilst at the summit the guests were received at the hotel which was decorated with white alpine roses and the music society played "Entry of the Gladiators".

The real reopening celebration took place later at the Kreuz Hotel in Brienz where President Grossmann of the Council welcomed the guests. The President of Thun, Johann Eduard Amstutz, mentioned the parishes of Lakes Brienz and Thun who as friendly neighbours had helped to raise the necessary finance in return for Brienz's contribution to the Lake Thun Canal in 1926. Dr. Born delivered greetings from the Provincial Chamber of Commerce, Herr Briner thanked the shareholders and Albert Eggler described how the finance had developed. Dancing was held after a performance by the local yodelling club. Even Roman Abt, whose patent rack system was in use by the railway, showed his enthusiasm.

The following day inhabitants of the Brienz area were granted reduced fares to travel up "their" mountain and almost 700 took advantage of this concession. A return trip, which had cost 16 fr in 1892, was fixed at 10 fr for 1931 but on this special day was reduced to 7.50 fr.

Once again railway foreman Viktor Rösti, with his workforce, was back in his old position supervising track maintenance. Viktor was respectively grandfather and great grandfather of his later successors on the line, Gustav Rösti and today's assistant depot chief Hansreuli Rösti.

The Next Twenty Years

In 1932 the share capital was increased by 100,000 fr and a new loco, today's No.6, was ordered for entry into service the following year. This was a superheated loco which SLM constructed by incorporating some components from a similar type of metre gauge loco. Together with two new carriages, which were ordered at the same time, the total cost was 91,000 fr. On 29th August the railway's conductors were issued with whistles and instructed in a set of whistle codes to assist them in giving directions to the loco drivers.

During the course of 1934 the management decided to improve some of the facilities which included an enlarged depot at Brienz and additional water columns at both Brienz and Planalp. During 1935/36 the old locos were converted to operate on superheated steam at a cost of 126,000 fr. This conversion, encouraged by the performance of No.6, resulted in water and fuel consumption figures being almost halved together with a reduction of 15 minutes in their uphill journey time. An order was placed with SLM for a seventh loco, of similar design to No.6.

Loco No.7 arrived in 1936 at a cost of 67,000 fr together with another two carriages for 17,775 fr. For the first time in the railway's history, on two Sundays crowds of people could not be found seats. The same year the path from the Rothorn to Brünig was opened thanks to a gift from the renowned patron of the Rothorn, Emil Aeppli of Zurich.

During 1940 loco No.2 was out of service awaiting new cogwheels and a total rebuild. On Sunday 25th August a loco driver had to be severely reprimanded for defying the orders of his conductor. Contrary to instructions he had brought his empty train down through Oberstafel loop and met a loaded train coming uphill at Chüemad, forcing the other driver to return to Planalp loop!

During Winter 1941/42 the Chüemad Bridge was once again damaged by an avalanche. In the Spring it collapsed and some parts were washed hundreds of metres down the gully. Because of the War steel was unobtainable, so a new 47 metres long wooden bridge was built at a cost of 65,200 fr. Made of oak and pine, this new bridge was designed to be removed for storage, clear of the avalanche path, each Autumn and re-erected the following Spring.

Despite the War, a financial surplus was made in 1943. About one month before the start of the 1945 operating season the slaughter of the Second World War finally ceased when Germany surrendered.

In 1947 a short cableway for supplies between the summit station and the hotel was built which replaced the use of wheelbarrows. Some 13 years earlier the hotel had been provided with its own diesel generator to provide electricity.

The BRB's history is notable for the amount of snow clearing work. In the railway's early years up to seventy men were used for this work which provided a welcome source of income to many families in Brienz. However it also created large costs which had to be debited from the Company's operating account. In 1951 a snow clearing machine was used for the first time and, after solving initial teething problems, mechanisation soon proved to be successful.

PASSENGER FIGURES 1931 - 1951

1931......27,013	/	1938......58,505	/	1945......53,049
1932......30,463	/	1939......30,635	/	1946......52,035
1933......36,972	/	1940......23,436	/	1947......67,806
1934......32,375	/	1941......31,893	/	1948......54,209
1935......38,761	/	1942......35,259	/	1949......72,258
1936......43,618	/	1943......39,269	/	1950......56,153
1937......60,711	/	1944......32,125	/	1951......61,335

13. No.6 with bogie carriage B16 and 4w carriage B26 crossing the former bridge at the upper end of Oberstafel passing loop. In the background above the train, the route can be seen climbing the Breitengrat slopes. Rothorn Kulm Station and the mountain's summit are just off the top left of this view, which dates from 1935. *(collection - Keith Taylorson)*

14. No.4 at Brienz waiting to work the 10.19am departure. Note the supplies of refreshments, alongside the station building, bound for the summit hotel. 4th July 1960. *(D.W. Winkworth)*

15. No.6 propelling an up train into Planalp. The train comprises two carriages, one 1892 bogie and 4 wheeled C26 (now B26), together with a 4w wagon used for conveying supplies and luggage to and from the summit hotel. By 1982 the set of points in the foreground had been removed and the headshunt, at the left of this scene, became part of an extended passing loop. 4th July 1960.

(D.W. Winkworth)

Chapter 8
THE ROAD TO RECOVERY

A Cableway ?

Management and staff alike were becoming worried by the likelihood of repairs to the newer locos. In fact, during 1953 SLM undertook a complete rebuild of No.6 at a cost of 40,000 fr. By the following year the first whispers of diesel operation were to be heard although it was generally realised that steam was a major attraction.

1957 saw the eighth successive season of poor weather. The Company decided that, whilst other railways were enjoying a boom, the cost of the BRB steam operation was becoming far too expensive.

For some time the managers had thought that eventually alternative forms of traction would have to be investigated because of the downturn in the railway's traffic. By 1958 some shareholders held similar views and so the Company President, Walter Kleiner of Regensberg, was authorised to make a detailed study of the costs of conversion from steam to diesel operation. Conversion to electric traction had been rejected because of the problems which would be faced by overhead catenary where the route was exposed to avalanches. The remaining alternatives were either diesel traction or replacement of the railway with a cableway.

Kleiner reckoned that the operating cost for a return journey to Rothorn by steam was 299.90 fr whereas the cost with diesel traction would be reduced to 190.90 fr. Five diesel railcars were envisaged and their cost, together with a storage tank for 20,000 litres of fuel, was estimated to be at least 2m.fr. Additionally a new Chüemad Bridge would have to be built and all the tunnels enlarged at a further cost of 370,000 fr.

Huldreich Ruede, who was a BRB director, was also authorised to examine the cost of a cableway via Sitschenen and Dirrengrind to the Rothorn. He reported back to the general meeting on 21st June 1958 that he was convinced that the railway, now in a poor state, could not be preserved for much longer and believed that a speedy decision was needed. He reckoned that a cableway carrying 400 passengers per hour could be constructed for 3.357m fr. This would have comprised two cabins, each with a capacity of 80 people, and a journey time of eleven minutes. Later a preference was shown towards the possibility of siting the valley station at Schwanden to the east of Brienz.

As a result of Ruede's report the Board of Directors unanimously agreed that the Company should introduce a cableway as soon as possible. An extraordinary general meeting was called without delay to submit revisions to the Articles of Association and to consider the financing and design of this project. The shareholders passed these proposals unanimously. It seemed that the end of BRB steam had finally been reached! However there was vehement opposition both within Brienz and throughout Switzerland .

The railway staff were particularly disillusioned and under loco driver Hans Hulliger, who was President of the Brienz section of the Swiss Railway Association, they demanded a meeting. This took place at the Schützen Hotel on Saturday 18th April 1959 where Ruede explained the project and extolled the advantages of reduced operating costs and increased earnings that the cableway would provide through greater carrying capacity. Brienz Council would also benefit by collecting more taxes. He said that the bold scheme would provide a cableway which would be the sensation of the era and provide a profitable substitute for the legendary Swiss steam mountain railway.

Ruede admitted that one problem had been raised by the Planalp and Rothorn farmers. They were opposed to the scheme because they would lose their only means of transport so they had been promised that a road would be built. He also told the employees that as many of them as possible would be employed by the new cableway and promised a satisfactory solution for the rest.

Although the projected cableway had its opponents Ruede said that when he asked these objectors if they would contribute financially to save the steam railway then they soon changed the subject of conversation! However his plan was seen by many natives and foreigners as the only way of retaining some method of transport for tourists to the Rothorn summit.

Hulreich Ruede gave lectures to railway societies in Basle and Zurich but in Brienz the wheels of progress turned very slowly. The project was making little headway and he advised the management that, no matter how long the deliberations, local people should remain patient. However there were some who believed that too much patience would result in an opportunity lost. He also criticised press reports which showed no desire to understand the railway and its operating problems.

It would be wrong today to condemn the proposed cableway. The railway's management had become worried as to how they could preserve the BRB. They saw a cableway as the only long term solution for maintaining a method of public transport to the Rothorn summit. This is understandable because at that time there was a boom in cableway construction and such investment would have provided the greatest profits with the least costs of staffing and maintenance. Had it been possible to convince the railway employees of the advantages of a cableway then the outcome might have been different but the project slumbered and the railway continued to operate with steam and further losses!

Business As Usual, Once More

In 1959 Willy Mathyer, the railway foreman, was injured by a heavy rockfall whilst working in Planalpfluh Tunnel. During 1961 a 150 cubic metres capacity water reservoir was constructed at the summit to supply the hotel. Loco No.1 was scrapped at Brienz after being found to be beyond economic repair.

A year later the timber Chüemad Bridge disappeared for ever after a life of 20 years. A new embankment with culvert under was constructed to one side and the line was slewed across onto its new alignment. Today trains have to slow for the sharp curve at this diversion and the stone abutments of the original bridge are still evident. After converting from steam to diesel operation, the Monte Generoso Railway sold a steam loco to the BRB for barely 40,000 fr including repairs. This replaced the former No.1 in the BRB fleet.

1964 was a successful year with a six figure passenger total for the first time resulting in an operating profit of 75,000 fr. Plans for a new cableway from Sörenberg up the north side of the Rothorn to the summit alarmed the management committee. Another record was created on 5th August 1965 when 1,593 passengers were carried. Following a large rockfall at Niederried on Lake Brienz in 1966, coal deliveries arrived one month later than usual. In 1967 the line's Diamond Jubilee was celebrated in a simple manner and a record figure of 111,465 passengers for the year resulted. In 1968 Swiss TV produced a programme entitled "With Steam & Folk Music" which made stars of both the railway and several village clubs.

16. No.7 entering Planalp with an up train of two bogie carriages. The leading carriage is C27, now the "Bistrowagen" B27.   4th July 1960.   *(D.W. Winkworth)*

The Second Cableway Proposal

Another cableway project was proposed in 1969 at a cost of 4.4m.fr. In contrast a fully re-equipped electric railway would have cost 10m.fr. Even foreigners from as far away as the USA were shocked to learn that the line was to be allowed to die.

Although no proper committee existed to represent people in the area around Brienz, the villagers made it clear that they were against a cableway and wished to see the steam railway preserved. However one small group which included Hannes Walz, engineer of Worb; Joseph Rösti, chief of BLS Thun & Brienz Lake Steamers; and Hans Schild, retired schoolmaster of Bönigen, sought and found prominent supporters such as Professor Franz Escher of Bern. He persuaded the Statesmen Schaffner and Bovin as well as SLM director Meyenburg to support their ideas. In order to get an idea of costs, firms who were in a position to build new locomotives were contacted both home and abroad. The idea was, that by introducing diesel locos, the old hard working steam locos would be able to enjoy an easier life.

On 28th November 1969 seven Brienz citizens led by Jakob Flück-Perren requested that the Parish Council should place the problem of the Rothorn Railway on the agenda for their next meeting. 282 people authorised to vote attended that meeting on 28th January 1970 and decided unanimously that the council representative who sat on the BRB Board of Directors should pass on their wish that rail traction should be continued. (The Parish Council held 2300 of the total 15380 shares.)

In contrast to the memorable general meeting of 1958, this cableway proposal failed completely. Steam enthusiasts vehemently defended continuance of the existing operation. All the previous resolutions to dispense with steam were now worthless! The Action Committee for the Preservation of Brienzer Rothorn Rail Operations resolved that 2.34m.fr should be spent on essential reconstruction and repairs over the next ten years.

Introduction Of Diesel Locos

In 1970, the State renewed the Company's operating concession for a further 50 years and a carriage underframe was purchased from the Monte Generoso Railway for 9,600 fr. Because of late snow, trains could only run as far as Planalp until 28th June.

During that year the railway supporters obtained budget costs for a new diesel loco together with a new depot which were estimated at 1.6m.fr. Now they had to consider how to obtain the necessary finance. The steam supporters posted hundreds of personal letters to their acquaintances. The fact that eventually 3.85m.fr was raised was thanks to the efforts of Walter Abplanalp, director of Reka Travel, who was also a former BRB director.

The railway profited from a good Summer in 1971 carrying 169,622 passengers which was another record! All too often it was becoming impossible to carry all intending passengers and so a new way of increasing train frequency was sought. The Company decided to construct their own prototype diesel loco and order new higher capacity carriages. In designing this first diesel loco, engineer Karl Bernhard had to find the answers to several problems including how power could be transmitted from the diesel engine to the drive pinions mounted on the two axles.

In this 80th year of the BRB's history the first significant accident occurred on 20th August when a high wind lifted a fully laden carriage from the rails above Oberstafel. Fortunately only minor injuries resulted.

In 1972 the share capital was increased from 3.852m.fr to 4.55m.fr and the first two of a total of seven new 56 seat panorama carriages built by SIG entered service. With minimal tare weight, roller bearing axles and curved sliding windows, their cost was 200,000 fr each.

At the end of April 1973 the first diesel locomotive No.8, designed and built by engineer Bernhard, was delivered. It was constructed at the Monte Generoso Railway depot at Capolago finished with Regazzoni bodywork, the family business of the former world champion motor racing driver Clay Regazzoni. After trial runs with works and goods trains the diesel entered public service, running with one of the new carriages, in the Autumn. With his construction work, Bernhard also helped the BRB survive a crisis and develop into today's flourishing undertaking. In October demolition of the old depot at Brienz with its turntable and roundhouse was completed.

By June 1974 the new depot was ready for use after seven months of construction. Following the prototype's success, a further two more powerful diesel locos, Nos.9 & 10, were ordered from the Ferdinand Steck Engineering Works in Bowil at a cost of 400,000 fr each.

These two diesels were delivered in 1975 and each loco was intended for use with two 56 seater carriages. With a crew of two, instead of three, an extra 64 passengers would be carried compared with the old steam locos!

PASSENGER FIGURES 1952 - 1976

1952......66,977		1968.....110,658
1953......69,599	1961......88,296	1969.....137,739
1954......58,752	1962......91,331	1970.....140,947
1955......63,878	1963......90,124	1971.....169,622
1956......68,321	1964.....106,009	1972.....147,813
1957......69,281	1965......95,336	1973.....159,930
1958......78,218	1966......99,527	1974.....140,556
1959......79,499	1967.....111,465	1975.....147,235
1960......72,754		1976.....153,309

17. Approaching Planalp on board a down train headed by No.4 which will run into the left hand track. Two trains are waiting on the "straight" side of the loop to proceed uphill.   4th July 1960. *(D.W. Winkworth)*

Chapter 9
TOWARDS THE NEXT CENTURY

An Eventful Decade

At an extraordinary general meeting on 29th October 1977 shareholders voted to increase the share capital from 4.55m.fr to 5.1m.fr to provide extra investment capital. The alternative was to take out further loans which would have only saddled the Company with interest payments. In 1979 the Company purchased 2.5 acres of land on the summit ridge from the Planalp Alpine Farming Co-operative. The Chüemad avalanche shelter was built using 600 tonnes of material which was brought to the site in 250 train loads.

The unsatisfactory facilities at Brienz station were redeveloped during 1980 for which both Brienz Council and the Canton made considerable contributions. During the Winter half a dozen BRB employees were found work at Meiringen airfield.

During snow clearing work on 22nd May 1981, a machine was catapulted by a snow slide onto the railway line but little damage was caused. However during blasting operations to clear snow the depot chief, Gustav Rösti, sustained serious injuries to an eye from a splinter of ice. Then on 29th June, 150 metres of track were covered by an avalanche which closed the route and put diesel No.8 out of service for a time.

The Schonegg avalanche shelter was built in 1982 necessitating 294 train loads for the 200 cubic metres of concrete and 60 tonnes of steel. This construction task, at 2150 metres above sea level, was carried out mostly at night. Also in 1982, working timetables were introduced and conductors were provided with uniforms. The following year the new Schonegg shelter was damaged by an avalanche and repairs necessitated another 141 cubic metres of concrete which was brought up by 156 trains and also by helicopter. On 14th May 1984 the 54 year old haulier Franz Zobrist of Brienz, who had provided a valuable snow clearing service for 19 years, was killed in a snow slide. It was the first, and hopefully the last, fatal accident in the BRB's history.

Because of poor weather the 1984 season was the worst for 18 years with only 128,007 passengers. In contrast 1985 was one of the best with 163,978 passengers providing a record turnover of 2.14m.fr. Oberstafel passing loop was lengthened by 80 metres. This was accomplished by replacing the small stream underbridge with an embankment and culvert wide enough for double track. In June transport of the five millionth passenger was celebrated.

The start of the 1986 season was delayed for some days because of overnight snowfalls which kept recovering the track after it had been cleared during the day. The first train did not reach the summit until Tuesday 10th June. By the year end passenger figures were 6% lower than 1985. During the year experiments were conducted using different types of coal in the steam locos. The results proved that a change of fuel would be worthwhile.

In 1987 diesel loco No.11 and two newly designed carriages, which in total cost 1.9m.fr, entered service. The carriage sheds were enlarged to house the new arrivals. However 1987 was the worst season for twenty years and snow was still being cleared from the line in July! The result was a loss of 176,500 fr for the year so once again the railway had to cope with a set back.

"Target BRB 2000"

In 1987 the Company embarked upon the largest investment programme in its history using the slogan of "Target BRB 2000". This defined how the BRB was to develop as it entered its second century. Important ingredients of the plan were the supply of two new steam locos, construction of a summit station building and renovation of the summit hotel. During 1987 the restaurant at the hotel was modernised with installation of a new buffet area and a lift. The terrace restaurant was extended to provide a covered area with 120 additional seats and the shop was considerably enlarged.

In 1988 the share capital was further increased from 5.1m.fr to 9.65m fr. The Canton contributed 2.7m.fr whilst Brienz Council granted an interest free loan of 300,000 fr. This extra funding enabled the Company to proceed with the order of a new oil fired steam locomotive, No.12, from SLM in Winterthur at a cost of 1.8m.fr. Delivery was arranged for early 1992 to coincide with the BRB's centenary celebrations.

There were further activities during 1988. The district schools of Baden and Wettingen founded "Swiss Environment Operation" and carried out maintenance work on the footpath between Oberstafel and Rothorn. Also between 12th and 23rd September about 50 "railway soldiers" held an exercise and undertook track maintenance. Furthermore a joint marketing organisation was founded together with Brienz Tourist Office and the Swiss Open Air Museum which had opened at Ballenberg in 1978.

18. No.7 leaving Planalp on an up train with a 1972 bogie carriage in which the perspex windows are closed
in the second compartment. July 1985.   *(P.Q. Treloar)*

The 1989 general meeting agreed to release 1.6m.fr for the construction of a new staff house and tourist
accommodation at the summit hotel. In 1990 the "Target BRB 2000" programme was granted a further 1m.fr for
more improvements at the hotel. The passenger figure of 182,848 for the year 1990 was the highest ever - an increase
of almost 8% on the previous best.

A new electric central heating system was installed during 1990 and by the start of the 1991 season the summit
hotel had three restaurants capable of seating 350 people and the sun terrace had seats for another 150. There were
48 beds in single and double rooms, 52 beds in 4-bedded and 8-bedded tourist rooms and a further 50 beds in the
two tourist dormitories together with a room available for up to 20 people for meetings or seminars.

During 1991 the rock face at the summit station was blasted out to provide room for constructing a passenger
waiting hall and staff rest room. This successfully completed the improvements planned for the summit.

The trials carried out in 1986 had proved that by firing the locos with loose coal, instead of coal briquettes, a
saving of up to 20% could be achieved. Instead of 450 kg, only 350 kg was consumed during each round trip. One
by one the steam locos were modified to use loose coal so that by 1991 the use of briquettes was discontinued.

The centenary of steam was triumphantly celebrated with the delivery in 1992 of a brand new steam locomotive
to work alongside its one hundred year old ancestors. No.12 was delivered to Brienz on 18th May 1992. The arrival
of the first new steam locomotive in Brienz for 56 years provided a worthy excuse to hold a village festival!

After successful initial track tests in the station area, braking trials revealed that the two mechanical systems
retarded too much. After some adjustments had been made these systems operated within the required regulations
which enabled full track trials to commence.

The Federal Bureau of Transport carried out acceptance trials on 5th June whereupon No.12 was officially
handed over for service. This speedy commissioning ensured that the loco was available well in advance for the
railway's centenary celebrations on 17th June when it was named "Bern". Unfortunately, for various reasons, No.12
was without its trained driver until later in the season. The loco did not really see regular service until August but
even so had completed over 625 miles by the end of the season. The publicity both for the centenary and the arrival

19. Nos.1 and 4 standing at Planalp, both with 1972 bogie carriages, on their way up the mountain. The loco crews oil round here whilst the train conductor fills the loco's water tanks. 11th September 1977. *(A.J. Pike)*

20. No.4 followed by No.1, both with a 1972 bogie carriage, roll down into Brienz. The carriage sheds are visible on the left but compare their length with the view in illus. 22. 11th September 1977.

(A.J. Pike)

21. No.7 beside the water column on the right hand of the two tracks into the loco shed. The carriage shed is on the right. 24th May 1992. *(A.J. Pike)*

22. No.6 standing on the right hand of the two tracks leading into the loco shed. On the left can be seen the loco shed entrance of the other track. To the right of No.6 is the longer of the two carriage sheds, the other one is hidden. On the far right the "main line" curves away under the loco coaling plant. Since this photo was taken the front of the loco shed has been extended across to the carriage shed. 24th May 1992. *(A.J. Pike)*

23. No.12 in service with a 1987 bogie carriage descending towards Brienz. 12th August 1992.

(Christian Lüber/SLM collection)

of No.12 ensured that very many extra train journies were needed during 1992. By the end of the year the number of passengers had exceeded 250,000 - a massive increase of no less than 38% over 1991!

Initial findings were that No.12 met the promises made by SLM. Indeed power output proved better than expected and single man operation is successful. This modern oil fired steam locomotive causes no environmental problems as tests have shown that emissions of carbon monoxide and nitric oxide are less than from a comparable diesel engine.

During 1993 No.12 continued to prove extremely reliable and not only saw service on practically every day of the season but recorded nearly the highest mileage of the fleet. As a result of this success, early in 1994 the BRB placed a firm order for another locomotive of the same design. Subject to SLM's other commitments, it is hoped that delivery can be effected by 1996. Consideration is also being given to ordering a third identical machine.

Prior to the 1993 season a second track was installed at Brienz station and the locomotive depot was extended to make room for the new locomotives. Given good weather there is every reason to hope that passenger figures around 200,000 could become a regular occurrence on the BRB in future.

Since 31st October 1891 when the first steam train reached the Brienzer Rothorn, the railway has often struggled to survive. During the last thirty years steam preservation has also been a struggle but today the railway is stronger than it has ever been. Finance has been raised thanks both to the support of many faithful shareholders and the help of the general public. Many steam supporters and loyal members of staff who have fought tirelessly, and often stubbornly, have gained their reward.......steam will survive on the Brienzer Rothorn!

PASSENGER FIGURES 1977 - 1993

1977.....147,307	1983.....162,883	1988.....160,015
1978.....153,179	1984.....128,007	1989.....163,916
1979.....146,609	1985.....163,978	1990.....182,848
1980.....151,654	1986.....153,943	1991.....181,592
1981.....155,945	1987.....133,214	1992.....250,845
1982.....155,249		1993.....160,013

24. With the Mühle Stream waterfall just visible above the loco, No.2 enters Geldried with a 1972 bogie
carriage.   20th July 1992.   *(Mary Arnold)*

25. Diesel loco No.9 waits with a 1972 bogie carriage under the shade of the trees at Geldried loop before
proceeding downhill.   22nd July 1990.   *(A.J. Pike)*

Chapter 10
THE BRB TODAY

Friends And Neighbours

The Sörenberg-Brienzer Rothorn Cableway (LSBR) opened in 1971 and ascends the mountain from the northern side. It has 2 cabins which each carry 80 people from Schönenboden to the Rothorn in 8 minutes. In its first years the LSBR made less profit than expected and struggled to survive but today the Company is financially sound much to the satisfaction of the BRB. Both companies have adopted a joint marketing slogan, "One mountain, two railways", and passengers can book through tickets with either Company.

At the end of 1977, through Professor Veda of Tokyo Transport Museum, close links were formed between the only remaining steam railways in both Japan and Switzerland. In 1978, with celebrations in both Brienz and Japan, declarations of friendship and co-operation between the Japanese Oigawa Railway and the BRB were signed.

Each railway realised that the other was virtually unknown in their respective country. Media coverage was arranged to publicise both railways to millions of people. After two visits by a Japanese delegation, the BRB arranged their first official return visit to Japan in 1983. The trip, which was advertised amongst shareholders and Brienzers, was so well supported that further visits were made in 1985 and 1990.

The Oigawa Railway christened a diesel loco "Rothorn" and the BRB's No.11 was named "Oigawa" during a Japanese visit to Brienz in 1987. The close contacts thus developed have ensured the BRB's fame in Japan. During the intervening years many publications and videos have been produced in Japan and an increasing number of Japanese now visit the BRB.

A general desire by the Swiss public to ensure that the BRB's historic operation is preserved for future generations led to an approach being made to the Company for recognition of a supporters' association. As further support and new initiatives are often necessary, the Company agreed to the idea. The "Association of Friends of the BRB Steam Operation" was formed in 1991 to support the continued steam operations by means of membership subscriptions, fund raising and publicity campaigns.

26. With Lake Brienz in the background, No.6 descends with bogie carriage B16 and 4w carriage B26 just below the Planalp road level crossing about 0.5 mile above Brienz.   2nd July 1991.   *(Author)*

Snow Clearance

As can be imagined the depth of snow on the Brienzer Rothorn each Winter reaches a considerable depth. In extreme conditions trains may not be able to reach the summit before the end of June. This may be hard to believe on a glorious hot August day when the only snow to be seen from the summit is on the high peaks of the Bernese Oberland! Prior to construction of the avalanche shelter at the entrance to the Chüemad tunnel, the cutting might have been buried by snow up to a depth of 65 feet.

In former years several weeks were necessary for snow clearance and all too often the work would be nearing completion when fresh snow falls blocked the line. Today 10 men equipped with explosives, picks and shovels assisted by a wheel driven Unimog snow clearing machine commence their task each year around the beginning of May. This machine can attack the steepest drifts clearing up to 1,450 tonnes of snow per hour. When necessary an electric current is passed along the rack so that the exact location of the track can be found with a current detector. Except in the worst conditions, it is now possible for the line to be cleared of snow in 1 week, a far cry from the days when 70 men had to struggle for some six weeks!

Train Control And Timetable

Nowadays the train service to Rothorn Kulm usually starts on the first weekend of June and continues until late October depending upon weather conditions at each end of the season. Although, only locally advertised, a service is often run only as far as Planalp for the Whitsun holiday weekend when this falls a week or two before the start of the official timetable which appears as table no. 475 in the Swiss National Timetable.

BRB Timetable valid from 5th June - 24th October 1993										
Train No.	1	5	7 +	9	11		13	15	17	19 *
Brienz dep	0805	0905	0935	1015	1115		1305	1415	1515	1615
Planalp dep	0830	0934	1009	1044	1149		1334	1444	1544	1644
Rothorn arr	0855	1000	1035	1110	1215		1405	1510	1610	1710
Train No.	4	8		10	12	14	16	18	20	22 *
Rothorn dep	0905	1010		1120	1300	1340	1445	1545	1645	1720
Planalp dep	0939	1044		1154	1334	1414	1519	1619	1719	1750
Brienz arr	1005	1112		1220	1400	1445	1545	1645	1745	1816
Footnotes:	+ From 1st Jul to 31st Aug * From 5th Jun to 26th Sept									
Operating Notes:	Train Nos.1, 11 & 22 (from 27th Sep to 24th Oct - Nos.1, 11 & 20) will operate daily. Remaining trains may only run if traffic demands. Extra trains will run in busy periods.									
Steam Operations:	Up to 8 steam locos are in daily service. Train Nos.5, 7 & 9 will be steam powered whenever possible.									

Alexander Lindner originally designed the railway to cope with an annual figure of 20,000 passengers using 4 train sets and only 4 trips per day. Today the railway can easily carry over 180,000 passengers in a year. On a fine day at least 30 trains may ascend the mountain. The published timetable allows for 9 trains per day in the peak season at approximately hourly intervals. However each departure may consist of up to 4 train sets and extra trains are frequent when passenger demands are high. When several trains run together all, except the last in the convoy, carry a green and white disc at the front indicating "another train following". The last train carries a similar disc at its rear to indicate "end of last train".

This level of traffic can only run under close supervision. Since 1980 the BRB has used a radio system by which each train conductor is in contact with the control office throughout the journey. This system provides the necessary flexibility for amending crossing instructions, delaying departures or arranging extra train movements. In addition to the radio system the BRB's duty controller records all movements on a graph so that he can quickly arrange extra trains at short notice when necessary.

All points on the line are manually operated, each lever having an indicator displaying the point setting to approaching trains. Train crews operate points at the crossing loops as required. Each loop has a straight through track which is used by trains in either direction when no crossing is to take place. When crossing, up trains keep to the straight track whilst down trains curve in and out of the loop. Thus when trains cross one another the rule of left hand running operates.

On busy days even the older steam locomotives can perform four round trips per day if necessary. Because tourists can reach the Rothorn by the LSBR cableway or by several footpaths, the BRB's traffic is not always balanced as regards uphill and downhill passengers. On the busiest days it is possible to see up to 4 empty trains proceeding uphill from Brienz around 5.00pm, after the last timetabled departure, in order to collect tourists from the summit.

Fares

Considerable savings on normal fares can be made by use of the various concessions available to visitors. These include Family Cards, Half Price Passes and Regional Holiday Passes available from SBB stations throughout the country. There are other reductions available for pre-booked parties. Furthermore BRB co-operate with other transport organisations to provide special through fares for mountain walkers wishing to use the railway as part of a longer excursion from other systems such as the LSBR to/from Sörenberg or the SBB to/from Brünig Pass. Normal fares for 1993 were:

Brienz to Planalp or Planalp to Brienz: 22 fr single; 36 fr return.

Brienz to Rothorn or Rothorn to Brienz: 36 fr single; 58 fr return.

BRB FACTS AND FIGURES

Length of Line	7.6km	= 4.71 miles
Height Climbed	1678m	= 5495ft
(from 566m = 1854ft to 2244m = 7349ft)		
Gauge	80cm	= 2ft,7.5ins
Rack System	Double toothed Abt	
Minimum Curve	60m	= 2.98 chains
Steepest Gradient	25%	= 1 in 4
Average Gradient	22.5%	= 1 in 4.4

Tunnel Lengths				Avalanche Shelter Lengths		
- Schwarzfluh	19m	=	21yds	- Chüemad	40m	= 44yds
- Hard	119m	=	130yds	- Schonegg	100m	= 109yds
- Planalpfluh	290m	=	317yds	**Passing Loop Altitudes**		
- Chüemad	92m	=	100yds	- Geldried	1019m	= 3337ft
- Schonegg I	37m	=	40yds	- Planalp	1341m	= 4391ft
- Schonegg II	133m	=	145yds	- Oberstafel	1819m	= 5967ft

27. No.3, sporting an oil lamp, standing on the "main line" alongside Brienz depot. The lettering towards the rear of the loco shows that No.3 was overhauled in 1961. The unidentified carriage appears to be a five compartment fully glazed bogie vehicle probably seating 40 passengers.

(John K Williams)

28. No.7 outside Brienz depot during coal evaluation tests undertaken by SLM in 1986. During these tests SLM also took the opportunity to obtain information needed to aid design of the new locos, hence the amount of electronic instrumentation equipment.

(Courtesy SLM)

Chapter 11
LOCOMOTIVES AND ROLLING STOCK

Steam Locomotives

Standard livery for the steam locomotives is mid green, although the exact shade varies from one loco to another, with pale yellow lettering. In outward appearances the locos are of 0-4-2 wheel arrangement but, as is usual for rack locos, the four wheels on the driving axles revolve freely. Drive is provided by two double toothed pinions, one fixed to each of the driving axles. The steam fleet can best be described as consisting of three classes being built in 1891/92, 1933/36 and 1992 respectively. The first two are designed for right hand drive whilst the latest machine is one man operated.

H 2/3   Nos.1 - 5

The four original locos were supplied by Swiss Locomotive and Machine Works (SLM) of Winterthur during 1891/92 and the first two, if not all four, were delivered in time to assist in the line's construction. These four were supplemented by another of the same class in 1912 when the Wengernalp Railway's No.1 was purchased following that line's electrification. This loco then became BRB No.5. To confuse matters further the BRB's present No.1, which was purchased in 1961, replaced the original No.1!

These locos' cylinders are mounted one each side of the boiler, forward of the water tanks. Motion is transmitted to the drive cranks via the vertically mounted rocking levers at the front end of the loco. These levers connect the upper and lower connecting rods and reduce the crank throw so producing the necessary gear reduction. Each loco is able to propel one bogie carriage carrying between 48 and 60 passengers.

No.1 Built 1891 (SLM 688)	BRB, scrapped 1961
No.1 Built 1892 (SLM 693)	ex GN;1941-61 MG;to BRB 1962
No.2 Built 1891 (SLM 689)	BRB
No.3 Built 1892 (SLM 719)	BRB
No.4 Built 1892 (SLM 720)	BRB
No.5 Built 1891 (SLM 690)	ex WAB;to BRB 1912

[MG: Monte Generoso Bahn   BRB: Brienz Rothorn Bahn]
[GN: Glion to Rochers-de-Naye Bahn   WAB: Wengernalp Bahn   ]

Service Weight	17000 kg	= 16 tons, 14.6 cwt
Unladen Weight	14000 kg	= 13 tons, 15.6 cwt
Cylinder Stroke	550 mm	= 21.65 ins
Drive Pinion Diam.	573 mm	= 22.56 ins
Carrying Wheel Diam.	653 mm	= 25.71 ins
Pony Truck Wheel Diam.	520 mm	= 20.47 ins
Drive Reduction (Rocking Lever)		= 1:1.4
Boiler Pressure	14 bar	= 210 psi
Total Heating Area	43.5 sq.m	= 468.23 sq.ft
- Firebox	3.5 sq.m	= 37.67 sq.ft
- Tubes	33.0 sq.m	= 355.21 sq.ft
- Superheaters	7.0 sq.m	= 75.35 sq.ft
Grate Area	0.66 sq.m	= 7.10 sq.ft
Boiler Capacity	1000 litres	= 220 gallons
Tank Capacity	1200 litres	= 264 gallons
Coal Capacity	550 kg	= 10.83 cwt
Indicated Power	230 HP	
Cost in 1892	42,000 fr	

29. No.7 standing beside Brienz station building. The main steam pipe can be seen
leading to the cylinder with its short connecting rod to the front end gearing system.
July 1985.
(*P.Q. Treloar*)

H 2/3   Nos.6 & 7

The design of these two locos incorporates some major components, including cylinder castings, from a similar metre gauge loco produced by SLM in 1929. Like Nos.1-5, they have cylinders mounted forward of their water tanks. Here the similarity ends however for the pistons are connected to a sophisticated system of gearing mounted at the front end of the loco below the smokebox. The gearing then transmits power to the coupling rods via the connecting rods. With their lower drive ratio these locos produce a noticeably more rapid exhaust beat compared to their older stablemates. Their extra power enables them to propel one bogie and one 4w carriage conveying up to 90 passengers.

No.6 Built 1933 (SLM 3567)   BRB
No.7 Built 1936 (SLM 3611)   BRB

Service Weight	20000 kg	= 19 tons, 13.7 cwt
Unladen Weight	16700 kg	= 16 tons, 8.7 cwt
Cylinder Stroke	400 mm	= 15.75 ins
Drive Pinion Diam.	573 mm	= 22.56 ins
Carrying Wheel Diam.	653 mm	= 25.71 ins
Pony Truck Wheel Diam.	520 mm	= 20.47 ins
Drive Reduction (Geared)		= 1:2.2
Boiler Pressure	14 bar	= 210 psi
Total Heating Area	36.45 sq.m	= 392.34 sq.ft
- Firebox	4.0 sq.m	= 43.05 sq.ft
- Tubes	26.0 sq.m	= 279.86 sq.ft
- Superheaters	6.45 sq.m	= 69.43 sq.ft
Grate Area	0.78 sq.m	= 8.40 sq.ft
Boiler Capacity	1050 litres	= 230 gallons
Tank Capacity	1500 litres	= 330 gallons
Coal Capacity	550 kg	= 10.83 cwt
Indicated Power	300 HP	
Cost in 1936	67,000 fr	

30. No. 7 standing outside Brienz depot.
(John K Williams)

The BRB celebrated its centenary simultaneously with that of its five oldest steam locos which, although still giving good service, are running as museum pieces at reduced loads interspersed with modern fully laden trains. These old locos struggle to achieve the summit in one hour, especially as 5 minutes have to be allowed at Planalp to take on water.

SLM Engineer Roger Waller was convinced that a modern oil fired steam locomotive would meet the BRB's need. He realised that in spite of their robustness the one hundred year old steam locos were beset by high running and maintenance costs. After conducting a survey among passengers it was clear that many were prepared to pay

31. SLM, Winterthur constructed a pair of inclined stands with rackless tracks for load tests at their works. A cardan shaft was used to connect the intermediate gears of two locos and here BRB No.12, left, is connected to OBB No.999.201. The latter loco is acting as a brake to provide a load for No.12. In the foreground can be seen the exhaust gas analysing computers. March 1992.   *(Courtesy SLM)*

slightly higher fares for their journey if steam was employed. Therefore at least some of the locos in use had to be steam and couple performance with economy. It was apparent that new steam locomotives were needed. He believed that this was the only way to maintain the line's attraction together with economic operation.

In 1988 BRB decided to order a new steam rack loco. The Montreux, Glion to Rochers-de-Naye (MGN) and Austrian State Railways (OBB) also made the same decision. SLM of Winterthur obtained the order for 3 prototypes, with options for 12 more, and took on the tasks of design and construction, which proved to be fascinating exercises. Already some data had been obtained from the fuel tests using loco No.7 in 1986, but over a thousand drawings and innumerable calculations were needed before actual construction could commence. SLM had to manufacture at least 80% of the components themselves.

The design of the new steam loco, incorporating the latest techniques and construction methods, enabled production of a modern machine which is far more economical in operation than the original locos. Construction incorporates modern all welded fabrication methods using materials unavailable when the original locos were built.

One immediately visible difference is that, unlike the earlier locos, No.12 has the cylinder block mounted directly below the smokebox. This allows a much improved pipe layout with a consequent decrease in throttling and temperature losses. Such innovations as roller bearings and a central lubricating system will assist in reducing running and maintenance costs. Fuel is low sulphur oil and, thanks to the incorporation of 3 independent braking systems together with a dead man's pedal and other safety devices, one man operation is possible. Conveyance of 40-60 passengers with the old steam locos requires a train crew of three (driver, fireman and conductor) whilst the new loco can convey 120 passengers with a crew of only two. The new steam loco matches the two hour round trip performance of the diesel locos. Further economies are achieved by using full thermal boiler insulation and an external electrical "plug in" pre-heater which can heat the boiler water of the cold locomotive without supervision. Together these facilities allow the loco to be quickly made ready for service, for example when traffic increases unexpectedly.

Service Weight	15700 kg	= 15 tons, 9.0 cwt
Unladen weight	13200 kg	= 12 tons, 19.8 cwt
Cylinder Stroke	400 mm	= 15.75 ins
Drive Pinion Diam	573 mm	= 22.56 ins
Carrying Wheel Diam.	653 mm	= 25.71 ins
Pony Truck Wheel Diam	440 mm	= 17.32 ins
Drive Reduction (Geared)		= 1:2.3
Boiler Pressure	16 bar	= 240 psi
Total Heating Area	43.23 sq.m	= 465 32 sq.ft
- Firebox	5.14 sq.m	= 55.33 sq.ft
- Tubes	24.86 sq.m	= 267.59 sq.ft
- Superheaters	13.23 sq.m	= 142.41 sq.ft
Firebox Floor Area	0.9 sq.m	= 9.69 sq.ft
Round Trip Fuel Consumption	160 litres	= 35 gallons
Boiler Capacity	1200 litres	= 264 gallons
Tank Capacity	1400 litres	= 308 gallons
Oil Tank Capacity	560 litres	= 123 gallons
Maximum Speed on 1 in 4	12 km/hr	= 7.44 mph
Length Over Buffers	6260 mm	= 20 ft, 6.5 ins
Width	2200 mm	= 7 ft, 2.5 ins
Height	3200 mm	= 10 ft, 6.0 ins
Indicated Power	300 kW	= 402 HP
Cost in 1992	1,800,000 fr	

32. BRB No.12, left, with OBB 999.201, right, in the assembly shop at SLM, Winterthur.

(Courtesy SLM)

Coal Supplies

The BRB loco fleet requires several different types of fuel. Still the most important, and that which causes most worry, is coal. Until 1990 briquettes were widely used. The only manufacturer, Werk Werister at Lüttich in Belgium, ceased production that year due to lack of demand.

Calorific Values of Fuel

Ruhr Coal	34200 kJ/kg
Werister Briquettes	33200 kJ/kg
Diesel Oil	42000 kJ/kg
Wood	13000 kJ/kg

During 1986 extensive fuel trials had been undertaken by SLM using loco No.7 to evaluate four alternative types of coal. Results proved that, whilst all these could provide sufficient steaming capacity, the most suitable was that available from the Ruhr in Germany. The test chief remarked in his report that he did not recommend the continued use of briquettes. Further trials confirmed the earlier tests and so 50-80 mm sized Ruhr coal has been used since the 1991 season. This decision led to some modifications of the locos and improvements to the railway's infrastructure.

The loco cabs were slightly altered so as to provide coal bunkers which could be filled through the roof. This involved redesigning the rear cab sheet on Nos.1-5. The original, almost full width, rear window openings were replaced by two individual openings, one on either side of the coal delivery space. As a result the rear of these locos is now similar to Nos.6 & 7 and the loco crews have better protection from poor weather on the downhill run.

During 1991 an efficient coal storage and loading plant was constructed over the departure track alongside the carriage sheds at Brienz. Today it takes only two minutes to load a locomotive with up to 800 kg of coal from this plant which is fed by a semi-automatic conveying system.

The fuels used during 1991 amounted to 305 tonnes of coal and 98,000 litres of diesel oil. These totals resulted in average fuel consumption figures per return trip of 350 kg for coal, including lighting up and stand by losses, and 76 litres for diesel oil.

Loco Maintenance

One hundred year old steam locomotives which are in daily service during Summer need careful maintenance during Winter. Professional experience is vital and many technical skills have been handed down through several generations of BRB staff. The men who perform this work today are proud of their knowledge and skill and now also undertake work for other concerns. The specialised staff comprises six engineers, four fitters, two electricians and an apprentice engineer. The most important maintenance work is regularly controlled by the Federal Bureau of Transport and the Swiss Steam Boiler Association.

Various maintenance tasks are carried out at planned intervals but about once in every 8 years each loco is completely rebuilt. Each Winter about 1200 hours are spent on maintenance and by Spring the locos are ready once more to transport passengers to the Rothorn. Passenger safety is essential and the various braking and control systems are examined carefully and renewed at regular intervals. Before returning to service each fully laden train set is allowed to run freely and when the brakes are applied the train must come to rest within 100 feet to meet safety requirements.

The BRB, being a single season operation, has many disadvantages but it does have the one advantage that the specialists, who carry out the Winter maintenance, become loco drivers during the Summer and so each one knows his own locomotive very well. This enables him to recognise any minor problems which may arise in service and, in many instances, to cure such faults without taking the loco out of service. In comparison to other railways therefore, locomotive availability is extraordinarily high.

33. **A century of SLM steam locomotive development. No.12 (1992) after delivery, but prior to naming, at Brienz in front of No.7 (1936) and No.2 (1891). May 1992.** *(Christian Lüber/SLM collection)*

34.   No.3 near the end of track beyond the station building at Brienz. The loco's cylinder is partially hidden by the "System Abt" plate. The rocking lever, which transmits the motion to the coupling rod, can be seen at the front end. Note the coal briquettes stacked beside the line; their use was discontinued after the 1990 season. July 1985.   *(P.Q. Treloar)*

35. Smoke boxes have to be cleaned at the end of the day's work. The task is eased somewhat by using the portable chute visible below the smokebox door. Outside Brienz depot in September 1975.

(A.J. Pike)

Diesel Hydrostatic Locomotives

In planning for diesel locomotives one of the major problems was finding a braking system which would minimise wear and tear during the downhill journey. On the steam locos this problem is overcome by the Riggenbach counter pressure braking system whereas conventional diesel vehicles have mechanical braking which is completely separate from the engine speed resulting in a high rate of wear on the brakes.

To overcome the problem the BRB decided to seek outside assistance to find a completely new system of braking. Extensive experiments and trials led to a diesel hydrostatic system which had never before been used by a mountain railway. The original diesel locos have been in successful service for almost 20 years and have stood the test very well. Despite the good operational experience gained, no other comparable mountain railway in the world has adopted the system which remains unique to the BRB.

The engine transmits power, at about 1600 rpm, via a distribution gear to two rotary axial pumps. An electro hydraulic proportional valve in each pump feeds the correct volume of oil to two closed circuit hydraulic motors which power the drive pinions through a gearbox. The driver can alter the speed of the loco by a lever which simultaneously controls the mechanical fuel pump and the engine revolutions. On the downhill run all the braking energy is passed through an oil cooler which dissipates heat to atmosphere.

The loco brake and the hydrostatic brake are supplemented by two other independent systems which are normally used as parking brakes after successful hydrostatic braking. However in an emergency these brakes can be used to bring the train safely to a stand.

The four diesel locos are all 0-4-0 machines and, like the steam locos, these carrying wheels are free on their axles. No.8, the 1973 prototype now rarely used on passenger trains, can often be seen on p.w. trains or supply trains to the summit hotel. The three production machines are each capable of propelling two of the modern bogie carriages containing 120 passengers.

The original livery for the diesels was brown cab with a broad yellow band separating the red frame from the black engine cover. In recent years the cabs have been repainted red and the black has been extended down over the area of the former yellow band resulting in a simpler but more striking colour scheme. Lettering is now white as distinct from the yellow of the old livery.

HM 2/2   Nos.9 - 11

No. 8 Built 1973 (Prototype)	BRB	
No. 9 Built 1975 (Steck Eng., Bowil)	BRB	
No.10 Built 1975 (Steck Eng., Bowil)	BRB	
No.11 Built 1987 (Steck Eng., Bowil)	BRB	
Service Weight	13550 kg	= 13 tons, 6.7 cwt
Drive Pinion Diam	573 mm	= 22.56 ins
Carrying Wheel Diam	653 mm	= 25.71 ins
Maximum Speed Uphill	14 km/hr	= 8.68 mph
Maximum Speed Downhill	12 km/hr	= 7.44 mph
Fuel Tank Capacity	450 litres	= 99 gallons
Length Over Buffers	5250 mm	= 17 ft, 2.7 ins
Width	2100 mm	= 6 ft, 10.7 ins
Height	3200 mm	= 10 ft, 6.0 ins
Power Output	660 HP	
Cost in 1975	450,000 fr	
Cost in 1987	1,000,000 fr	

Carriages

The carriage livery is bright red with white lettering although some of the older vehicles still display the earlier pale yellow lettering. There are several carriages still in use dating back over fifty years and some to the railway's opening. This collection includes 4w, 6w and bogie vehicles carrying between 28 and 48 passengers each. Most of these older vehicles still have canvas blinds although the use of such carriages in poor weather conditions is now unnecessary.

Carriage Nos.B1, B11, B12 & B21 survive from 1892:-

B1 is the remaining 6w carriage and seats 40 passengers. B11 & B12 are identical bogie carriages each seating 48 passengers in six compartments. B21 is a unique 4w carriage with seating for 28 passengers; it comprises two fully glazed compartments with a total of 16 seats plus a covered section seating 12 passengers and which is open above waist height at the uphill end - ideal for fine weather journies.

Carriage Nos.B16, B26 & B27 all date from 1933:-

B16 is a six compartment bogie carriage seating 48 passengers and is often paired with B26 which, although a 4w carriage with seating for 32 passengers in four compartments, is of matching appearance. B27, a bogie saloon carriage with seats for 40 passengers, has five large windows on each side. This carriage originally had balconies at both ends but at some time was rebuilt with a fully enclosed lower end and converted into a "bistrowagen" for special parties. Passengers now have to enter from the balcony at the uphill end. These three carriages have a slightly higher and more curved roof line than that of the earlier stock.

All 1892 & 1933 built carriages have an open balcony, with roof, at the uphill end where the train conductor stands for control of the hand brake in any emergency.

In 1972 new bogie panorama carriages were introduced. Their design provides bench seating for 56 people in 7 compartments with waist height doors and bodywork. Above this height the window frames curve inwards resulting in an overall vehicle shape somewhat reminiscent of a London tube train. Within each of these frames there are perspex windows which slide down from the roof for protection when required. The conductor's position is fully enclosed and separated from the passenger section by a glass screen. Constructed by the Swiss Industrial Co. (SIG) of Neuhausen, there are seven of these carriages in service numbered from B3 to B9.

In 1984 the Company decided to acquire two new carriages. Purchase of such items was relatively difficult as suitable products could only be obtained to special order because, apart from the different gauges and rack systems in use, different railways have different requirements. The main problem lay in how to accommodate as many passengers as comfortably as possible within a vehicle of low tare weight. This was accomplished by using modern methods of construction which incorporated as few components as possible with regard to cost.

After studying various alternatives it was decided to proceed with the plan prepared jointly by Steck Engineering of Bowil for the running gear and Ramseier & Jenzer of Biel for the bodywork. The carriages were successfully tested in February 1987 before entering service as Nos.B14 & B15. Initially they were used singly with steam locomotives Nos.1-5 but, as intended, they are now used together with new steam locomotive No.12.

The new carriages are far more comfortable than any of the previous ones and each has a centre gangway and individual seating for sixty passengers. Their fully enclosed design with large windows and sliding doors means they are ideal for use in the poorest weather conditions.

Carriage Nos.B14 & B15 Technical Data.

Length over Buffers	12200 mm	= 40 ft
Bogie Centres	6500 mm	= 21 ft, 3.9 ins
Width	2190 mm	= 7 ft, 2.2 ins
Height above Rail Level	2840 mm	= 9 ft, 3.8 ins
Unladen Weight	4000 kg	= 3 tons, 18.7 cwt
Laden Weight	8500 kg	= 8 tons, 7.3 cwt
Seats	60 passengers	
Cost in 1987	450,000 fr	

Carriages are not coupled to the locomotives, the continuous gradient being sufficient to keep the buffers in contact on the downhill journey. The SIG and Ramseier & Jenzer carriages are fitted with air brakes but this system can only be used when these vehicles are paired with a loco so equipped - a diesel or No.12.

Non-passenger rolling stock consists of two 4w open goods wagons and a hydraulic crane bogie wagon. The wagons are now used mainly for p.w. work whilst the crane is used both for track maintenance work and for loading and unloading the station rubbish containers.

36. A diesel loco with two 1972 bogie carriages awaits passengers at Brienz. Note the perspex sliding windows and the air brake pipe for use with diesel locos and more recently with No.12. 13th October 1989.
(A.J. Pike)

CARRIAGE FLEET SUMMARY

Built	Fleet No.	Wheels	Seats	Notes
1892	B1	6	40	5 compartments; fully glazed/droplights
	B21	4	28	2 glazed compartments + open section
	B11/B12	Bogie	48	6 compartments; blinds
1933	B26	4	32	4 compartments; blinds
	B16	Bogie	48	6 compartments; blinds
	B27	Bogie	40	"Bistrowagen" saloon; blinds
1972	B3-B9	Bogie	56	7 compartments; sliding perspex windows
1987	B14/B15	Bogie	60	Enclosed fully glazed saloons

Note - All carriage interiors are open above waist

37. A close up of the buffing arrangement between a steam loco and a 1972 bogie carriage. There is no air braking system on the steam locos, except No.12, so the pipe cannot be linked. The carriage runs uncoupled from the loco.   24th May 1992.   (A.J. Pike)

38. SLM "official" drawing of No. 12 and (below) an extract from the press release announcing the order for this locomotive. The data sheet appears on page 54. *(courtesy SLM)*

INFORMATION — SLM

8 Mai 1991

Schweizerische Lokomotiv- und Maschinenfabrik
Société Suisse pour la Construction de Locomotives et de Machines
Swiss Locomotive and Machine Works
8401 Winterthur, Schweiz
Tel. 052-264 10 10, Telex 896 131 slm ch, Fax 052-23 87 65

Steam Rack Locomotive, Type H 2/3

The Austrian Federal Railways (ÖBB), which operate rack railways on the Schafberg and the Schneeberg, the Brienz—Rothorn Railway (BRB) and the Montreux—Glion—Rochers-de-Naye Railway (MGN) each ordered in 1988 one prototype of the newly developed steam rack locomotive, type H 2/3. Since these rack railways are mainly used by holiday-makers, the external appearance was intentionally made closely similar to that of old steam locomotives.

These oil-fired steam locomotives are suitable for one-man operation and are provided with deadman's and vigilance safety devices. Due to the new operating concept, 120 passengers per train can be transported by a two-man crew, i. e. engine driver and conductor. Formerly, a three-man team was required to transport 60 to 80 passengers.

Full thermal insulation of the boiler results in a further improvement in economic performance, since minimum heat loss occurs during standstills. An external electric preheating device enables heating up of the cold locomotive without supervision, and guarantees instant readiness for service. A sudden increase in transport demand can thus be dealt with more readily.

The steam locomotives have three independently acting braking systems. A Riggenbach back-pressure brake serves as wear-free retarder. Spring-operated block brakes acting on the cogwheel axles and spindle-operated band brakes acting on the crankshaft function as mechanical stopping brakes.

Delivery of the first locomotive is scheduled for 1991.

Full Steam Ahead into the Future

Modern Steam Locomotives from SLM

Steam locomotives are always a fascination for young and old. They attract numerous passengers, as in the case here with the new SLM steam locomotive of the Brienz Rothorn Railway.

economic

- One-man operation
- Oil-firing, eliminates fire-cleaning
- Insulated boiler, reduces stand-by losses
- High efficiency
- Low operating costs
- Instant readiness for operation

friendly to the environment

- Lowest CO and NO_x emissions
- Reduced consumption of energy
- Low lubricating oil consumption

attractive

- Appealing to the public
- Classical appearance
- Romantic journeys
- Visible mechanics

Thanks to the modern SLM steam locomotives, attractive, viable steam services are possible again, even where steam traction was endangered or regarded as a thing of the past.

Thanks to the oil-firing system developed especially for the new SLM steam locomotives, the driver is able to perform the duties of the fireman as well.

One-man operation

The modern SLM steam locomotives have no rivets. The frame, the cab, the boiler, cylinders and water tanks are integral welded structures and designed according to the latest state of the art.

Visible technique

The welded boiler is completely insulated. This minimises stand-by losses.

After a day's operation, the modern SLM steam locomotives are quickly and without any overnight heating ready for service the following day. An electrical pre-heating device is available for heat up from the cold state.

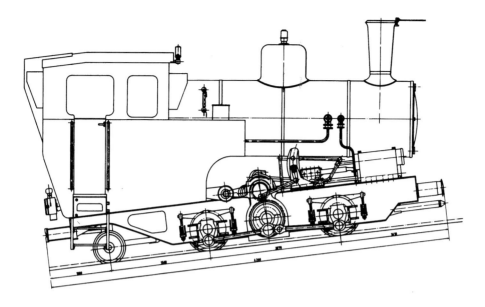

Daten	ÖBB	BRB	MGN
Spurweite	1000 mm	800 mm	800 mm
Länge über Puffer	6260 mm	6260 mm	6260 mm
Größte Breite	2200 mm	2200 mm	2200 mm
Größte Höhe	3230 mm	3200 mm	3200 mm
Zahnraddurchmesser	573 mm	573 mm	573 mm
Tragraddurchmesser (neu)	706 mm	653 mm	653 mm
Laufraddurchmesser (neu)	493 mm	440 mm	440 mm
Radstand total	3650 mm	3650 mm	3650 mm
Radstand fest	2070 mm	2070 mm	2070 mm
Kesseldruck	16/18 bar	16/18 bar	16/18 bar
Zylinderdurchmesser	280 mm	280 mm	280 mm
Hub	400 mm	400 mm	400 mm
Übersetzung	1:2,3	1:2,3	1:2,3
Gewicht	16 t	16 t	16 t
Vorstellast:			
bei 250‰ Steigung	17 t	17 t	—
bei 220‰ Steigung	—	—	20,5 t
bei 200‰ Steigung	23,5 t	—	25 t

Data	ÖBB	BRB	MGN
Gauge	1000 mm	800 mm	800 mm
Length over buffers	6260 mm	6260 mm	6260 mm
Overall width	2200 mm	2200 mm	2200 mm
Overall height	3230 mm	3200 mm	3200 mm
Cogwheel diameter	573 mm	573 mm	573 mm
Carrying wheel diameter (new)	706 mm	653 mm	653 mm
Pony wheel diameter (new)	493 mm	440 mm	440 mm
Wheelbase, total	3650 mm	3650 mm	3650 mm
Wheelbase, fixed	2070 mm	2070 mm	2070 mm
Boiler operating pressure	16/18 bar	16/18 bar	16/18 bar
Cylinder diameter	280 mm	280 mm	280 mm
Stroke	400 mm	400 mm	400 mm
Gear ratio	1:2.3	1:2.3	1:2.3
Weight	16 t	16 t	16 t
Load capacity:			
at 250‰ gradient	17 t	17 t	—
at 220‰ gradient	—	—	20.5 t
at 200‰ gradient	23.5 t	—	25 t

Für vollendete Fortbewegung
Pour la locomotion parfaite
Locomotion at its best

Chapter 12
THE ROUTE DESCRIBED

Brienz Station

The BRB station in Brienz is situated 1854 ft. above sea level on the opposite side of the road from the SBB Brünig Railway station and the Lake Brienz landing stage. The original wooden building is of typical Swiss chalet design consisting of the station offices, with a gable facing the road, together with an open waiting hall. The latter is covered by a roof supported on posts decorated with consoles of a double curved design.

In 1935 the building was extended at its eastern end. At the same time the main access at the western end was moved enabling the station office to be extended by 2.4 metres into part of the original waiting hall. In preparation for the 1992 centenary the building was restored as far as possible to its original condition. At the same time the ticket office facilities were improved and an archive store created. The restoration work cost 85,000 fr and was financially supported by the Lakes Thun and Brienz Safe Banking Society together with donations from Brienz citizens. As a result the building has been made a protected structure.

Until recently the rail facilities at Brienz Station comprised a single track at a ground level platform with water columns for the locomotives. After substantial excavation of the hillside a second track was installed in time for the 1993 season. The new track forms a loop, approximately 100 yards long, extending uphill from the upper end of the station platform. This layout has eased train operations considerably.

Brienz Depot

Within the length of the loop, but from the original track, two sets of points lead left into the depot. The first set leads to the locomotive depot and one carriage shed whilst the second set leads to another carriage shed. Each of the two carriage sheds, both of timber construction, contains two tracks.

39. **Brienz Station building as restored to its former glory in 1992. To the right is the extension which was added in 1935.**
(Courtesy BRB)

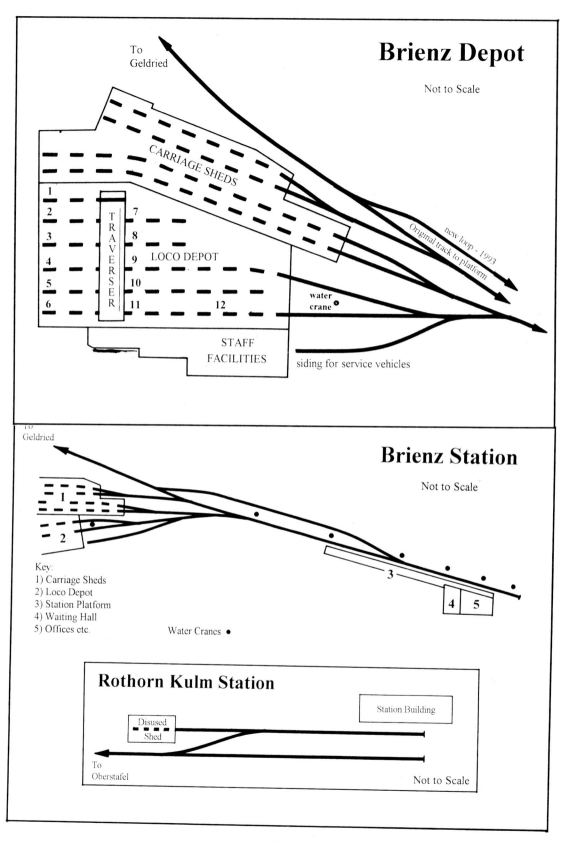

Brienz Depot

Not to Scale

To Geldried

CARRIAGE SHEDS

TRAVERSER

LOCO DEPOT

1
2
3
4
5
6

7
8
9
10
11

12

water crane

new loop - 1993

Original track to platform

STAFF FACILITIES

siding for service vehicles

Brienz Station

Not to Scale

To Geldried

1

2

3

4 5

Key:
1) Carriage Sheds
2) Loco Depot
3) Station Platform
4) Waiting Hall
5) Offices etc.

Water Cranes ●

Rothorn Kulm Station

Station Building

Disused Shed

To Oberstafel

Not to Scale

40. This view of Brienz depot shows four locos being prepared for work on 12th August 1961 - from the left they are Nos.5, 7 & 4 together with No.3 which is standing on the "main line". The former round house loco shed, which was demolished twelve years later, is visible in the left background. Rail access to this shed was by means of a turntable positioned in the track beyond No.5. A further loco of the original type, just visible in the shed doorway on this track, is probably No.2 because the original No.1 was scrapped in 1961.   *(John K Williams)*

Furthest from the main line is the modern locomotive depot which can be entered on one of two tracks. Inside the building, much of the floor area is sunken with the tracks supported on metal frameworks to ease the task of locomotive maintenance. Although only two tracks enter the depot, there are six parallel tracks inside accessed by a traverser. This system enables the locomotives to be placed well apart with good all round access for servicing. The front of the depot was extended during the 1992/93 Winter in order to provide space for storing further locos in the future.

Brienz To Geldried

The main line climbs immediately from Brienz and, with the depot on the left, trains pass under the modern coaling plant as the line curves to the right and heads north alongside the Tracht Stream. A minor road is crossed on an underbridge and the houses on the outskirts of the village are soon left behind. At 0.4 mile the Tracht Stream and a footpath are crossed on another underbridge. The line now traverses open meadows, crosses the minor road to Planalp on the level before entering Wang Forest and curves left towards the north west at 0.6 mile. The route maintains this general direction through the forest for a further 0.6 mile passing through the 21 yards long Schwarzfluh Tunnel en route. A long right hand curve through a cutting turns the line east. Leaving the forest trains again cross the Planalp road on the level before entering Geldried passing loop which is picturesquely set amongst a few deciduous trees and open meadows.

Here, at 3337 ft. above sea level and 1.35 miles from Brienz, watering facilities are available. To the right there is a glorious view over Brienz village and the lake. Above on the left hand side the towering Planalpfluh cliffs, through which the line has yet to climb, dominate the scene. Indeed regular visitors can pick out the two "windows" in the rock face through which their train will shortly pass. To the left of these "windows" the spectacular Mühle Stream waterfall plunges down the cliff to the valley below.

41. The attractive scene at Planalp looking up the track. Inside the wooden building train times are displayed alongside the ticket office, at the left side of the covered shelter, and the toilets are to the right.   4th July 1960.   *(D.W. Winkworth)*

Geldried To Planalp

Leaving Geldried trains continue eastwards through the meadows before curving left through 180° to enter the 130 yards long Hard Tunnel whence the line emerges in a westerly direction to climb a ledge through the forest along the cliff face. Some 1.75 miles from Brienz the line enters Planalpfluh Tunnel on a slight left hand curve. This tunnel is 317 yards long and its left hand wall is broken by the two large "windows" from which superb views to the south of the high snow capped peaks of the Bernese Oberland can be seen across the blue water of Lake Brienz. Passengers can also glimpse the passing loop at Geldried now over 600 feet below the train, seemingly a model railway! Upon leaving the tunnel the line curves right to the north and follows the Mühle Stream, which is out of sight through the trees over 250 feet below on the left. The forest begins to recede and meadows appear above the line on the right when unexpectedly trains enter the halfway station of Planalp at 4391 feet above sea level and 2.23 miles from Brienz, about 30 minutes travelling time.

This station, which has a small wooden waiting shelter incorporating a disused ticket office, serves the nearby summer hamlet of Hausstadt where there is a mountain restaurant. The passing loop is well used and steam locomotives take on water during the uphill journey. The surrounding meadows provide a popular area for picnicking at the lower end of the wide south facing valley with lovely views towards the Jungfrau. Children can amuse themselves playing in the stream which runs close to the railway at the upper end of the station.

Planalp To Oberstafel

Leaving Planalp trains climb northwards along the side of the valley with the Mühle Stream still on the left. Higher up on the left can be seen the avalanche fences on the Tanngrindel slopes. The valley is typical Alpine pasture land often resounding to the sound of bells from the herds of cattle in the valley below and on the hillsides above. Across the valley, hikers on the path from Planalp to Rothorn have a good view of the passing trains. Some 2.75 miles from Brienz the line turns towards the north east, passing Mittelstafel farm buildings above on the right, and shortly afterwards the Mühle Stream is crossed on the Chüemad Embankment. The abutments of the former bridge,

42. No.4 taking water at Planalp with 10.19am train from Brienz. Note that there appears to be a four man train crew; in fact one of these is probably the station master. In the foreground can be seen a point lever with its indicator for drivers of down trains. 4th July 1960.   (D.W. Winkworth)

which was demolished in 1962, can be seen on the left as trains round the sharp curves of the embankment. From here the line goes through a series of reverse curves in open country before trains enter the Chüemad Avalanche Shelter which protects the cutting at the lower end of Chüemad Tunnel. The total length of these two structures is 144 yards, some 3.1 miles from Brienz. The line leaves the tunnel in a south easterly direction clinging to a rocky ledge with a view back down the valley towards Planalp on the right hand side. The line follows the hillside, curving generally to the left, until a right hand curve brings trains into Oberstafel passing loop where there are watering facilities.

The loop is situated 3.56 miles from Brienz at 5967 feet above sea level. The slopes of the Brienzer Ridge rise behind the train whilst the summit station at Rothorn Kulm is visible high above on the left. In front is the forbidding rocky face of the Dirrengrind.

Oberstafel To Rothorn Kulm

Leaving Oberstafel, and for the next 0.8 mile, the line curves to the left through 180° as it climbs around the foot of the Dirrengrind. Crossing the Breitengrat slopes, now facing west and with the terminal buildings still visible but on the right, trains enter the Schonegg Avalanche Shelter. This shelter is 109 yards long and adjoins the 40 yards long Schonegg I Tunnel. The line then curves sharply to the right and briefly emerges into daylight before entering the 145 yards long Schonegg II Tunnel. Trains re-emerge into daylight facing east and pass a small shed on the left before reaching a set of facing points which lead to one of the two dead end tracks of Rothorn Kulm Station.

Rothorn Kulm Station

The left hand track immediately has a set of trailing points for the siding leading to the stone built shed. Originally this building was used to store a train overnight so that, in the event of an emergency, guests or hotel staff could be taken down the mountain. The shed remained in use until about 1965. However once the LSBR cableway was completed in 1971 there was no longer any need for the BRB to provide this emergency standby and

43. A train comprising loco No.6 with bogie carriage B16 & 4w carriage B26 at Planalp Station. With the permanent way looking newly ballasted, possibly after the line's reopening in 1931, and showing rolling stock which was not purchased until 1933, this scene probably dates from 1935 at the latest.

(Collection - John K Williams)

44. No.12 with the two 1987 carriages B14 and B15 climbing away from Planalp over the footpath crossing at the top end of the station.

(Courtesy BRB)

45. Ancient loco and modern carriage with the jagged Dirrengrind as a backdrop. Oberstafel loop is also visible. *(SVZ/W. Storto; courtesy SNTO)*

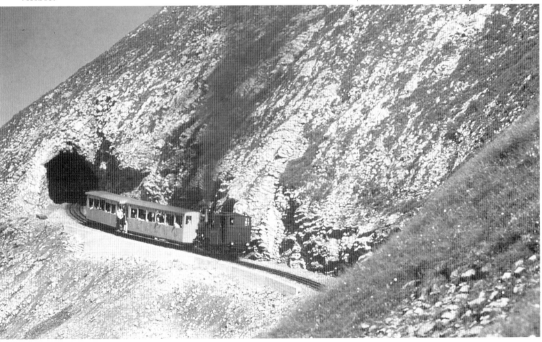

46. It has not been possible to obtain this view of a train entering Schonegg I Tunnel since the avalanche shelter was constructed along this ledge in 1982. *(Giegel; courtesy SNTO)*

47. **No.4 at Rothorn Kulm waiting to leave with 11.25am train. The hotel can be seen above the carriage whilst the actual summit is hidden by the wooden shelters. At some time after the date of this photograph, but certainly by 1977, this set of points was removed and the track in the foreground was truncated in front of the nearest wooden building. During 1991 the rockface alongside the train was blasted away to provide the area for the new station building. 4th July 1960.** *(D.W. Winkworth)*

today the siding is only used to hold an extra train waiting to depart when traffic is very busy. The station is 4.71 miles from Brienz and 7349 feet above sea level and the journey will have taken just over an hour. Over 1300 feet below can be seen the passing loop at Oberstafel, only 0.6 mile away as the crow flies but 1.15 miles by train.

Until 1991 the summit station was a terminus with no adequate passenger facilities. This presented no problems in good weather but when the weather changed suddenly it became very unpleasant for waiting homeward bound passengers. The BRB decided that, as facilities had not changed since the opening of the railway, this should be rectified as a matter of some importance under their "Target BRB 2000" investment programme. After much planning, during which the Canton boundary of Berne and Lucerne had to be altered, the new station was constructed during 1991. The building is set back into the rock face at the northern end of the site providing essential improvements for both staff and passengers. There is now covered shelter for about 100 people and the flow of arriving and departing passengers has been improved. The building also includes a ticket office, modern toilet facilities and a comfortable staff rest room.

Views From The Summit

But the visitor, enthralled as he is by the railway journey, must not fail to walk the half mile to the summit of the Rothorn and marvel at the beautiful views to be seen in every direction. On a clear day in the north, across the Mittelland and the Jura, one can see the Black Forest and Vosges with their mountain chains dividing the Rhine levels. From Mount Säntis in the north east a panorama stretches round through the peaks of Glarnerland, Central Switzerland and the Bernese Oberland towards Les Diablerets in the south west. When the cloud base is low the passenger may be fortunate enough for his train to emerge into sunshine near Oberstafel. Then the panorama from the summit will be even more dramatic with the mountain peaks pointing upwards through a sea of cloud.

48. A busy scene at Rothorn Kulm. On the right hand track No.7 stands in front of diesel loco No.10. Three more trains are standing on the left hand track headed by No.5.   11th September 1977.

(A.J. Pike)

49. The stone built shed at Rothorn Kulm, which was formerly used to store a train overnight, is now no longer used. 4th July 1960.

(D.W. Winkworth)

ACKNOWLEDGEMENTS

This work is my first to be published and my thanks must go to Plateway Press for accepting my manuscript. Encouraged by this, and with the need to obtain photographs and further information, I requested and received help from the following individuals:-

Sarah Farnham, my niece, who despite her busy work schedule found time to translate letters into the German language for me.

Les Heath, former Membership Secretary of The Swiss Railways Society, who was good enough to deliver a copy of my correspondence to Brienz when I was experiencing difficulty contacting the BRB through the postal service. Also it was Les who suggested that I contact Alan Pike, then Chairman and now Vice President of the Society, as a source of photographs.

Herr E. Streule, Director of Brienz Rothorn Bahn AG, who could not have been more helpful in answering my queries or more generous in providing me with plans, photographs and information.

Herr R. Waller, of SLM's Steam Locomotive Department, who was kind enough to provide me with much information and photographs - particularly regarding the development of their modern steam rack locomotives.

Evelyn Lafone, of the Swiss National Tourist Office in London, who willingly provided me with brochures, maps and photographs.

Peter Treloar, D.W. Winkworth, Brian Stephenson, John K Williams and Alan Pike, who have provided many of the photographs without which the production of my book would have been that much more difficult.

David Gander who drew the maps.

Last but not least Mary, my wife, who enjoys visiting the Brienzer Rothorn as much as I do and who even photographs the occasional railway subject!

To all the above my very grateful thanks.

50. Beauty and the beast! The mountains of the Bernese Oberland provide a backdrop for the silhouette of No.2 standing at Rothorn Kulm.
(*Courtesy BRB*)